Rambling

& Wandering

Zachary Peterson

This book is a culmination of what I've learned about myself in my first year of sobriety. Here's to the future –

Acknowledgments:

To be honest, this section by itself could probably be an entire book. The order of appearance does not mean any more or less importance than the next.

Mom, I owe you a letter, so I'm going to write you one here. Thank you for being such a strong warrior throughout my entire life. You are a rock star.

Ashley, you are one of the strongest people I know, thank you for being so brave and inspiring me to get help.

Grandma Savino, your diary pages were the hardest to write, thank you for being you.

Jess, you could not have been better with all of your inspiration. You are a shining light in my life.

Austen, Lambda School, I have no words. You have changed my life in a way that I could only express in a book.

Grandma Oakley, strong like bull.

Aunt Roxy, you just know.

To everyone in this book, thank you so much for teaching me everything that you have.

Table of Contents:

Introduction……………………………………………..007
Preface………………………………………………...011
1. Welcome to Rehab…………………………………017
2. Kia Ora………………………………………………..019
3. Aesthetic Ethics……………………………………022
4. Day One……………………………………………029
5. 12/10…………………………………………………..035
6. Day Two……………………………………………039
7. 12/11…………………………………………………..048
8. First Step, Fail…………...…………………………051
9. Day Three…………………………………………056
10. Game Over. Try Again?…………………………...061
11. Day Four…………………………………………067
12. 1,000 Words………………………………………076
13. Day Five……………………………………………078
14. next()………………………………………………..084
15. Day Six……………...………………………………089
16. Free Falling…………………………………………095
17. Enter Stage Left……………………………...……098
18. Sweet as……………………………………………105
19. Day Seven…………………………………………...108

20. HTTP Error Code 409..………………………………..110

21. Finding Sobriety…..…………………………………...113

22. Day Eight.…..………………………………………….116

23. The Bond.…..………………………………………….120

24. Day Nine.…..…………………………………………..124

25. Keyframes…..………………………………………….125

26. Signal.…..…..………………………………………….130

27. The Pin.…..…………………………………………….134

Afterword…………………………………………………..138

Introduction

This book is going to be strange.

Like me, the structure is probably going to be a little off, and that's how I want it. There are many moments of trauma, so if you get super invested in the characters this is probably not the book for you.

I will make you laugh. I will make you cry. But unfortunately that's how the real life healing process goes. The beauty in recovery is that it's perfectly imperfect. Words that hurt me are in here. There is no Voldemort, so I'm not going to sugar coat it.

In this story I portray almost every character in the sense that I have learned from these moments. I am both the hero and the villain of this story. I gave away the end, but the middle is the most beautiful part.

Sometimes our inner monologues show us who we really are as people, and some times that person can be ugly. I've only edited for brevity in certain places, leaving grammar untouched in others, all to keep the messages clear. All of the references in this book come from outside journals and writings that I've kept over the years.

There will be multiple content warnings throughout the book. They will be noted as such:

CONTENT WARNING

Reasoning*

* Reasoning will be replaced with the appropriate content label

Through my writing you'll learn about tech, life, and most importantly what it's like living with the silent enemy of PTSD, co-occurring bi-polar.

Excerpt: "It shouldn't be surprising, but there are actually people here I have more in common with than I thought. People that have also been through traumatic experiences that brought them near/close to death. There's a lot more people with PTSD here than I ever could have originally imagined."

So many of us deal with PTSD silently, forgetting about and/or struggling through our mental health. This book is for you. I hope it brings you hope, a bit of happiness, and most importantly a moment to heal.

Rambling

& Wandering

Preface

Debugging PTSD, Diagnosing your code

"Inside every large program, there is a small program trying to get out."

- C. A. R. Hoare

Computer Science is very similar to life. At different times you're faced with complex problems. Dealing with people who have ranging skill levels. Confronted with numerous languages. With more than 23 million web developers representing 7.8 billion of the world's population, we have a reasonably good representation.

Languages in Computer Science alone can be sub-categorized. Used in different manners, or even be general abstractions based on another language. Our understanding of each language's inner mechanics not yet fully realized, rabbit holes in their respective senses.

Seemingly, sometimes the easiest way to fix a significant problem is to have a non-functioning application. All of the flaws suddenly become apparent; errors get thrown, the console screams.

Therapy and debugging are similar in this sense. By actively engaging, you have a deeper understanding of your mental state, your code. You gain an idea of where you could potentially run into issues in the future.

You have the chance to reflect on what choices you've made that led to mistakes in the past. In both situations, your efforts being directly related to the outcome. Ironically, my initial understanding of computers and the human brain are what got me to this point. On occasion, life leads you to a specific location.

You show up searching for one thing but leave with that and so much more. There may be some things in here that are a little uncomfortable, but they're my truth.

ABSTRACTION: "the quality of dealing with ideas rather than events."

For example, take a car. You have the car, and you know it works. But you have no idea how it works. Without expert knowledge, you can't look at a vehicle and know each mechanical event that occurs.

In computer science, by using abstraction, you reduce complexity. Are you frequently running into the same issues? Maybe it's best to look past the generalizations and into the actual tech.

Using that same lens, you can look into your actions. Perform a dive deep into why you do the things you do. Explore the various ways you're wired. Simplified generalizations that you can cluster together.

Lambda School officially endorsed me as a Full-Stack Web Developer on November 20, 2020. An online coding school that I learned about on my way home from rehab, in the middle of a pandemic. Little did I know, I had already caught coronavirus.

It's more of a symbolic ending but obviously, leads up to this point. Lambda School, the online coding school, managed to further my coding skills with a life-altering lesson.

Schedule wise, the school's units are taught similarly to the way you build an application. Begin with the wire-frame, deciding on individual placements, and setting a styling theme for your containers. Before you begin the application, you undoubtedly already have something to show.

Set-up is followed by the logical portion, building out the application's business logic, a way for your application to live its life cycle. Finishing each unit, you're taught testing. Ensuring everything is behaving according to plan. A time to reflect, make changes and improvements.

Each of these phases, when combined, create a final product, similar to how we choose to present ourselves. We set how strict our morals will be and embrace our spirituality as to why. When Lambda School teaches HTML and CSS, the beginning blocks of the web, they stress the importance of this alone being all you need to start developing. HTML alone setting the stage.

Historically applications are built out farther, though. HTML tags just set the structure and contain the content. A separate CSS file is then added for color changes, font-styling, sizing. Anything you can imagine is visually creatable with CSS.

All by themselves, HTML and CSS are tools that can develop meaningful applications. Written correctly, a few files of "bare-bones" code doesn't strictly mean no impact. With the correct accessibility, structuring, styling, and data, you can potentially create something that changes the world. In Histography's case, they've managed to cover the last 400 years of what's happened here.

When applying similar generalizations to yourself, you gain a sense of self-awareness. Personal history will remain the same, but it's all about the way you present it. A person can't change where they're born. But they can say they're from an area around it. As Upstate New Yorker's, we tend to distinguish ourselves from people in NYC. Upstate alone is enormous, and a lot of city/town names are similar.

By just giving specific pieces of yourself, you can alter your impact.

Beyond that, where you live isn't constant. Where you're born may be definitive, but life lets you move anytime. One object with similar information, but multiple pieces of your life—your proudest details presented first.

A location will always be a location, much like how a body will always be a body. You're born predisposed to certain conditions, with particular features, and even assigned a gender at birth.

Simultaneously, though, they have no real value other than insight into where a person has been. By acting as a personal life database admin for yourself, you control your personal information.

My name is Zachary Peterson. I was born on September 5, 1993, in Elmira, New York. I'm a recovering alcoholic diagnosed with PTSD, and bipolar 1, who also happens to be gay. When I was 12 years old, I was blown up in a house. By 16, I'd had my second heart surgery, and at 18, was drugged and raped, followed by spending three and a half years in a physically and emotionally abusive relationship. In New Zealand, at 25, I experienced a city in lock-down because of a mass shooting. Altogether I've lived 15 of 27 years disassociated in some sense.

Factually correct, terribly presented, inaccessible.

Starting with HTML and CSS as building blocks, you can present all sorts of information, your truth, in your way. But the ability to speak does not make you intelligent.

I'm reclaiming my time.

1 — Welcome to Rehab

> "She generally gave herself very good advice, (though she very seldom followed it)."
> - Lewis Carroll

Monday morning! Which I'm hearing is the actual start to the program for new patients, or at least the ones who were admitted on Friday past a certain time.

Not one of my favorite starts of the day being woken up at 6:00 am to get blood work, but this will give me some much needed info on where exactly my enzymes and everything stand.

At the same time though, this is one of the first times in a long time that I've been able to wake up and drink a cup of coffee while watching the sun rise. A pleasant reminder that sometimes in life the small things really do matter.

Normally around this time I'm just getting ready for bed. Now I'm up, have eaten and am writing. Also got to take my medicine's because I was luckily in line before Big Guy the counselor came in.

Back to the reality of rehab though, we haven't even hit 8:30 am yet and there have already been two fights between residents and one between a resident and counselor Big Guy.

We've also lost TV privileges until 5:00 pm tonight because two of the residents were fighting about the news.

Which personally I don't understand, we all lose out because one woman watching the news and the angry guy that told her she wasn't allowed to watch the news. Although he had only been in the rec room for all of five minutes before the entire fight started. Who knows though I think we're all a little crazy in here.

This is quite possibly the first time I've ever felt my bi-polar actively acting up. I'm starting to get used to not being listened to at groups at this point, but also starting to talk more and more, so people are starting to listen. For whatever reason, this time just really annoyed me and I could feel my mood instantly change.

Thankfully the second meeting I got to participate in more. We spent time sharing what we were going to focus on in the next month. My answer was to try and be less quiet and try to involve myself more.

Apparently, I'm not the only person in the block (although she's a counselor) that's spent time homeless.

2 — Kia Ora

> "Be alone, that is the secret of invention; be alone, that is when ideas are born."
> - Nikola Tesla

Sometimes you meet people that come into your life for no reason other than to change it drastically. For me, those people are the ones I tend to call best friends.

I met Sweet on a cruise.

"Want to be his date for the night," some strange woman asked awkwardly?

"Sure," Sweet responded.

Throughout the extent of our brief date that night, he always reminded me how cute he thought my sister was. Here we are on a cruise ship in the middle of the ocean.

Disembarking sobered up, I was embarrassed by the night before. Sweet, on the other hand, had no problem coming up and reintroducing himself. We traded Facebook info and started following each other on Instagram.

Somehow we kept in touch for weeks after the cruise while I was in the pre-launch phase of New Rome Realty and New Rome Media's filming project. Both of which Sweet was tantamount in figuring out logistics for.

While I was in Virginia visiting my mom, we got the idea for him to come to the United States and be my assistant. All of which was contract-based. Sweet has dual citizenship in the United States and New Zealand because his mom is from here, while his father is from there.

In our adventures, we thoroughly demolished a room before putting it all back together. Sweet helped out in various ways, but his number one role was being a friend around the house.

Sweet did have a thing for my sister. My sister having a thing for him as well. At the time, she had a boyfriend, though, so it all wasn't possible. Otherwise, I'd probably be calling him an actual brother. Their largest high jinks amounting to a dethawed tray of shrimp in the upstairs bathroom mid-renovation. They both say they never kissed.

One week of our time together, we visited New York City; Sweet was obsessed with the idea of visiting the touristy sites with me, as I'd never been. We saw the Empire State building and a bunch of other places using the city pass touristy thing you can buy. Sweet's favorite was the Natural History Museum; he has something for electrical science.

At some point during our week stay, I went to Harlem for Kava with a friend. It worked out because Sweet wanted to see the New Yorker Hotel in person. He's obsessed with Tesla and told me all about the pigeons and the idea that the New Yorker was the perfect home base.

After the trip, though, it was time to let Sweet go, I didn't have enough money or enough for him to do. His main goals would have stemmed from Beyond Adversity, but I was on hiatus from working on that project.

Sweet and I stayed in constant touch, and on that same trip to Virginia, where it all started, I had heard from an Uber driver how beautiful New Zealand was to visit. She had spent two weeks there and said that she could have spent even more time there.

3 — Aesthetic Ethics

> "All you need in this life is ignorance and confidence, and then success is sure."
> - Mark Twain

My concept of ethics began with Star Wars. My Uncle Jer and I waiting in line to see Episode 1: The Phantom Menace at the midnight release, I was anxiously excited to be staying up so late. Darth Maul was the perfect red and black horned representation of evil in all of the commercials. While Anakin was so much more complicated, I could see myself in him.

Dreaming of Jedi was easy with my Uncle Jer, because in my mind he was one. Uncle Jer would always be playing around with computers, taking them apart and putting them back together. Little did I know I was drawing inspiration for a future career in software development.

Growing up I had an interest in learning all sorts of new things. My Uncle Jer was just one of my many inspirations. While at Lambda School, I spent a majority of my time learning JavaScript. Something they teach is a language of variables at heart.

In just one of the many lessons, you learn to interact with Application Programming Interfaces (API's). There's even a Star Wars API that you can interact with freely.

Much like in life, data in an application is easy to manipulate. You can split unnecessary or unwanted information from inputs/outputs. Allowing you to display slices of data you select and assign.

As a creator, you maintain access to your code. Although the next person you let touch your code could deconstruct what you've created. Time and energy are excellent deterrents. But to even deconstruct, one must be in public view. GitHub allows you to upload your repositories but designate whether public or private.

Life doesn't tend to be so fair.

In my preteen years, I was incredibly imaginative. But that was a side of me. I only shared with my cousins. That was private. At school, I was a soccer player. I played soccer year-round, training at MLS camps during the summer, playing fall, indoor, and spring seasons. That's who I was in public.

When I didn't have practice, I would spend my weekend with my cousins at my Aunt and Uncles house. The amount of time spent on their trampoline in far off worlds rivaled the complete Magic Treehouse Series. And our adventures in worlds didn't necessarily end when I went home. We could stop and pick them back up the next time.

The eldest of my two cousins acted in a database administrator role while we played. He would push events, people, or new data into the system, spontaneously altering the world at random points in time. Elaborate event chains we'd call back on. We'd not necessarily have the same output.

In the Star Wars Universe, the characters, too, are continually evolving. But in the API, they're static. Your only option to programmatically create dynamic applications is to do more than just present data.

In our games, our younger cousin was typically our version of Jar Jar Binks, whatever world we were visiting. Our clumsy, well-meaning sidekick. Every adventure needs one. Now and then, I would get read-write access to our character's flow. Padawan becomes Master kind of stuff. With JavaScript, you can programmatically do the same thing.

Using the Star Wars API, Jar Jar could all of a sudden become a Jedi from Hoth. It's all about what you display. What's manipulated. How much is real, is all your selecting to show that's true a name?

What could I be? Anakin, Darth Maul? Light side, dark side?

Original Xbox RPG Star Wars Knights of the Old Republic was my original playground. Over time you gain companions that are influenced by your actions. Different conversation choices you make with them directly altering how they continue. Saving before essential conversations, I could try different routes. Get new outputs. But no matter which path you followed, you always ended up doing the same things.

Light side story lines are more comfortable to build relationship levels—dark side edgier, pushing boundaries.

Character Defect: I hate finishing things because it kind of feels like the characters die; I've never gotten past the unknown world.

December 9, 2005, was an average winter Friday, school, then home. For whatever reason, though, my mom and I had made set plans for that night. Usually, that would happen naturally, but my mom wanted to spend that night together.

At some point, though, I decided I wanted to go to my cousin's house and spend the night.

I don't remember being at their house, just that it would be the start of a new weekend adventure. My cousin and I would create a world, and the experience would begin. In an unfortunate series of events, though, that world started itself. At 5:02 am, the neighborhood tremored, my aunt and uncle's house exploded.

"Much of the damage from the explosion was still evident Sunday. While pieces of the disintegrated home had been swept from the street, sheets of plywood, wads of insulation and other debris hung from tree branches."

In programming, it's like someone else is in control of your system, firing an infinite loop of events rendering the user unable or unaware of a way to exit. The dot Hack franchise inspired a fake world I was creating and writing about during my summers at camp; just like in the dot Hack franchise, the player/character would be stuck in a system that they knew was unreal.

After the house exploded, I don't remember waking up, ever really. I remained in a medically induced coma for seven days. While I was dreaming of a bright farm, I'd been airlifted from Arnot hospital to Strong Memorial two hours away. At first, I was only allowed to wake up on occasion to have my vitals checked.

Each time I woke up, I had to be retold what was happening, just to be put right back to sleep. My first question was making sure everyone was alive and doing okay. I followed by asking about the house.

Of my seventeen days in the hospital, I only have bits and pieces of memories. Memory fragments more similar to individual nodes with no links than a chain of events I was experiencing.

At some point during my stay, I developed a fever. At first, no one knew, as the nurses only came in to check on me during rounds, and it's not as if I was there for the flu.

While watching Law and Order SVU, my mom went into the bathroom and changed her sweatshirt. By the time she came out, my fever had spiked. Unknowingly hallucinating, I watched my mom exit the bathroom and asked who she was. The new sweatshirt, mixed with her appearance, didn't match my memory. My mom's always been my role model and one of my fiercest protectors. At that moment, to me, she was unrecognizable.

Wheeled away, they found a perforated colon.

Spared from the burden of a colostomy bag, we spent Christmas that year in the hospital. Two hours away from home. Overall, seventeen days split between the ICU and a room shared with my cousin that had suffered just as traumatic of injuries. Without MadLibs, I'm not sure any of us would have survived.

One stipulation of me being allowed to leave the hospital was that I had to walk at least once, and I was allowed to use the help of a walker. Without question, the longest time I'd spent not playing soccer, and here a few feet was going to be difficult.

New Game. Save.

4 — Day One: 5 Days Sober

> "You have to uncover to recover."
> - Unknown

Yesterday evening I finally arrived from Helio in Binghamton to Arms Acres in Carmel, NY. The trip took about eight hours, and three different vans to get here.

Within the first few minutes of arriving, a fight practically broke out and I realized how close to NYC I was. My initial thoughts were that this wasn't the place for me.

Admissions was packed, and with the van rides alone, I was completely overwhelmed. I mean, one of the other patients seeking treatment was making a drug deal on the way to the facility. At one point he even asked me my drug of choice.

"Whatever you need, I've got you," he said.

After finally getting to my assigned room, which took a drug test, strip search and even a wanding like you get at the airport; the stories my roommates were telling me terrified me. Stories talking about heroin, and a million slang words I had never heard before.

Finally after falling asleep, I got to meet the rest of the "block". Which gave me an image as if I was in a prison. Given the set-up of the facility it truly isn't that far from one. Even more fights were started at Breakfast and it wasn't even 8:30 am.

Our first group meeting of the day was about spirituality, luckily I'd made friends with one of the two roommates, the other kept insinuating that because I was gay I was going to try to get into his pants.

"Sabrina, baby," he said, cuddling up with an extra pillow.

Before the spirituality meeting began, the roommate that I'd gotten kind of close with pulled me to the side and asked me a question.

"When you go to the liquor store and you pay for whatever it is you wanted to buy do you think that's the final payment?"

"Sort of," I responded. "But you know you'll be back for more."

"Is that really all you're going to be paying for though," he pushed back.

Thoughts kind of escaped me at this point and he just let it simmer.

When it was finally our "blocks" turn to have speakers on spirituality he was the first one to speak. He phrased the question in the same kind of way, but instead of asking for answers, he explained it.

"Yes, you're paying whatever dollar amount for that bottle, or those cans. But what about the other things? Relationships, your health, your bills, or God forbid driving under the influence and killing someone," he said.

A simple question, but one with a much more complex meaning than you would think.

Quite a few of the speakers during spirituality raised extremely interesting points and posed insanely complicated questions. Questions and points that will ultimately help to living a sober life.

After spirituality we went back for some recreational tine, where the whole fight cycle started all over again. Feeling as if the location wasn't right for me already I needed a phone call; I'd requested one before spirituality but the counselors hadn't arrived yet. Thankfully by now they had.

Totally by chance, the counselors door I knocked on happened to be my case manager. Explained with no hesitation everything I was feeling and how different where I came from was.

In the few short minutes I was talking to her she completely understood everything I was trying to express. We tried to make the phone calls but due to the area code difference and random number there were no answers.

Thankfully the counselor had an alternate suggestion. Transferring to a smaller block with less people. To approve the transfer she had to get a confirmation from her supervisor.

In the meantime, I had time to fill before my first ever alcoholics anonymous meeting. First choice was obviously the library on campus. Found an oldie but goody by a great author "Grapes of Wrath" by John Steinbeck.

Granted with how loud the entire building has been since I've gotten here, I'm only on page seven.

Probably ten cups of coffee later, it was was time for AA. Which sadly pretty much everyone took as a joke, no surprise there was another fight.

Apparently it's quite common for the scheduled AA speakers to just not show up. So instead of an actual meeting we just went around the circle said our names and a high/low for the day. Aptly, it's hard to see how a fight could start here, but apparently anything is possible in this place. (My high was that it was my first day here and my low was that it was hard to fill my time.)

Pro-Tip: One of the counselors said that coloring mandella's not only fills your time, but helps with the recovery process, something about the design.

After we'd all gone around the circle it did break down into a sort of discussion. A recovering alcoholic shared a story about realizing that sometimes you have to let your inner-boy out. Which from what I gathered was just letting your emotions out.

Another man began to add on to what the original guy was saying and a few people started talking over him, cue the fight.

"Excuse me," he said.

And apparently those are fighting words. The situation devolved for all of a good five minutes before the probably fifteen minute total meeting was over.

More cups of coffee, a page and a half of "Grapes of Wrath" and back to the room for a nap. 'D' block was actually pretty great at first. Everyone was far more welcoming, and unlike the other blocks in the building it's the only co-ed block.

People introduced themselves right away and my two new roommates seem a lot more friendly. The room is a little bit smaller, and the setup is a lot different.

When I first got to 'D' block is when I really started writing, so for a majority of the time I just listened to what was going on around me; until dinner.

Although it's a co-ed block, men and women still eat separately in the cafeteria. So the women went first followed by the men. As soon as the girls got back one of the girls started talking about how she almost went off on some girl that said something.

No surprise, when the guys got to dinner we were only about five people in before a fight started right in front of me. Easily enough resolved, but just the sheer amount of fights in one day, so far, it's astounding.

Seriously out of no where Father Knowledge started a fight about social security and disability. Half of the participants trying to get a word in edge wise with a guy still a few years off of retirement.

We once again had to have a counselor come in and break it up. Not once, but twice. It had to be at least seven interruptions before it got back to a conversational tone.

Wrapping up the night though, with a pizza party none the less. I'll probably have gained a good twenty-five pound by the end of this stay.

5 — 12/10 - Sat.

At approximately 8:15 am, Steph called to say there was an accident an explosion and Zach was injured. When I heard this I had to sit down. As I wept I realized Ashley was there and I could hear her voice over and over again asking me what was the matter. This was a very hard thing to say and the not knowing how he was-was killing me. She instantly broke down crying. Everyone tried to comfort her and this was very hard when you're feeling so much pain yourself.

Jason and Missy came over and they too along with Kayla were weeping. The family stayed together just talking about how absolutely wonderful Zach is. I wished many times today that I could change places with Zach. He's twelve-years old and has his whole ahead of him. We then later got a call from Steph saying Zach would be okay. However, he was being transported to Rochester (Strong Memorial).

[…]

I was in the process of making arrangements to go there when we received another call saying they didn't know if Zach would make it. The shock of this had me hysterical. I felt like I had lost it. Jim and I were both only here in body because we were going crazy. Just at this point my sister showed up. She prayed with me and talked for what seemed a long time however it was only minutes.

She had us pack our bags and offered us her car as ours had no heat. We left for Rochester.

[...]

When we got there we met Steph, Jeremy and Shannon along with Emma. We all comforted one another. Before we left we had Jim call Billy Graham + assoc., 700 Club, our pastor, a friend from Syracuse, my sister, his sister, brother, and many others to start praying steadfastly.

In Rochester – we all talked about how precious and kind Zach is. I know God will hold him in his hands. After much wait the Dr. came in and explained the many injuries Zach had. The most present danger was possible injury to the aorta valve and trauma to the brain. I held Emma and rocked her to sleep, that seemed to comfort me as well as her.

John and Jeanette came from Syracuse with their pastor. He prayed for Zach. We stayed and got to see Zach. I know he will be alright because Jesus is holding him. We left around 6:00 pm Saturday night to come home.

6 — Day Two: 6 Days Sober

> "We are all in the process of becoming."
> - Audre Lorde

So many of the things that Mrs. Rose said made sense. Things that I'd honestly have never listened to had it not been coming from a stranger and being in the environment I'm currently in. Damaging relationships that you'll never be able to fully repair.

My first thought immediately went to my mom. There happens to be a sign in the D block that says something along the lines of "Children learn from a parents actions, not their advice." I've been doing my best not to show too much emotion since I've been here, but my first instinct after seeing that and hearing Mrs. Rose speak was to cry.

For years I've blamed my mom for her addiction. Multiple times accusing her of being hooked again using. That's not to say she hasn't relapsed a time or two, but every time she's gong through something doesn't automatically mean she's using again. Instead of trying to understand her emotions, I've always rushed to anger. Not because it was right, although sometimes justified, but because that was the easier response for me.

The number of fights that could have so easily been avoided. The amount of time that's been lost because my addiction had just consumed me. I honestly don't think there will ever be enough ways to apologize.

What should have been a motivation for me to change I was using as a crutch to be able to continue what I was doing to myself, to hell with the consequences.

Side note: Write a letter to mom

Even considering my relationship with my dad and Shannon over the years, it was so much easier to blame them for the things I was doing to myself. Thinking about not only the time lost with them but the time I lose with the girls as well. At this point my relationship with Shannon has been completely destroyed.

One of the only good things in regards to them is that after five years of only a few texts here and there we actually have an open line of communication again. It may have only been two conversations so far, but any step in that direction is a good one.

At this point, I've been drinking for so long the people I need to make amends with goes on and on. You never really see the damage that's been done until you're way down the road.

Once Mrs. Rose's lecture was over the guy's came back to the block where the girls were finishing up with spirituality. We then played a round of rehab Jeopardy. Embarrassingly, I know nothing in the end about rehab. It of course once again got heated. Still unsure how Jeopardy of any kind gets heated, but people were yelling over each other trying to answer. People getting pissed off about people raising their hands, all sorts of stuff.

I also found out that quite a few people in this unit have been in rehab a number of times. One guy having been in and out of jail and rehab for the last twenty years.

Completely off track in regards to what has been happening in rehab, but I'm realizing every day more and more how lucky I really have been throughout my life.

I've also realized why they give us art supplies and kids coloring book pages; for one it fills up time, two it's calming and helps limit the number of fights. Not that it works extremely well, because there have definitely been two more since I last wrote forty-five minutes ago.

Still don't fully understand why the fight started other than that "church lady" changed over the laundry for one of the guys and he felt it would have been better if she had asked first; despite the fact he originally asked her to do it for him? It's all a little confusing to me. The second one was because a guy asked another one of the unit guys to grab him a cup and proceeded to reach over his food. Which at some point in time someone will need to explain to me.

Dinner was fairly uneventful again, other than that I now think I have someone to sit with for meals. Still have no clue what his name is, but we actually talked more tonight, It feels kind of nice to know that there's someone else in here that is actually doing his best to stay out of the drama.

For it being only 6:00 pm. I'm actually really tired and haven't even taken my melatonin yet.

Seemingly there's nothing left to do or the night so now is probably a good time to describe the two units I've been in. I didn't really spend much time in 'A' block, but can still remember it fairly well. I wholeheartedly believe they make 'A' block as ugly as it is because they know there's going to be fights, and things are going to get ruined.

You start in a long hallway that branches off into the recreation room through a door to the left or a hallway to the right where more clients, as they like to call us, have their rooms. The main hallway continues to the case managers offices with another long hallway to the left that leads to med pass.

Pretty much all of the rooms here are similar in setup, maybe a small variation in what furniture is available in each room. The beds are actual beds, but they're green plastic covered mattresses. There's a mix of different options, like some have armoire's, others dressers, desks, each one is different.

'D' unit is much simpler in set-up. It's kind of shaped like the letter U. The recreation room is smaller but it's also a lot nicer with a constant supply of art supplies, whereas 'A' only had the lovely old lady Kate to hand them out.

Tonight was the first time where we actually got to share thoughts with our group and I'm really proud of myself. Instead of just sitting and listening to everyone else speak I shared with them what I shared with the entire block of guys. Now people in the unit actually know my name.

While in group we also covered positive communication skills as well as the obstacles that stand in the way of them. A lot of these are obstacles I could really relate to; low self-esteem, perfectionism, shame, dishonesty, lack of boundaries, aggression, passivity. I could easily write a few paragraphs on each.

Low self-esteem: For a long time I overlooked what my true value to people was. I haven't seen many of my good qualities in such a long time that in a lot of ways I forgot I even had them. I'll get glimpses of them every now and then but then in the back of my head my addiction tells me that was a one-off, that there really wasn't much to be proud of because there's no way I could keep up that pattern of doing things like that, so why even try? Beyond just that I put a dollar amount on what an hour of my time was worth. Forever on the internet with the fear at some point someone who I don't want to see it will.

Perfectionism: Practically everything in my life that I know another person will see has to be absolutely perfect, the way I speak, present myself, everything has to be put together in just a certain way for me to feel comfortable even trying to leave the house. I'll throw myself to the side just so that I can make other people think I'm perfect to a certain extent. Granted when my drinking kicks into over drive I tend to let my guard down a bit, and some of the things I normally try to hide from people come pouring out.

For the last lecture of the night I went to my first NA meeting and we finally had an outside speaker from an outside actual NA home group. He spoke about how although he's never been to an institution/rehab, he has been down the hill.

One of the biggest pieces of advice he kept repeating over and over again was to read the literature, and to remember that although there is AA alcohol should still be considered a drug and NA is in general for addicts.

Possibly one of his best quotes of the night was that "you weren't using the drugs, the drugs were using you." And honestly he was an inspiration. Last Thursday was eighteen years sober for him. Which honestly is hard to imagine given that I've been drinking for thirteen.

As soon as I do get out, my first goal is going to be both an AA and NA meeting as soon as possible as well as finding a group. The groups solely in hopes that I can find a sponsor or in this case sponsors. A church so that I can have a large support system and start trying to re-find my faith.

Ever since college when studying philosophy in general and ethics, spirituality and religion have always really interested me. At some point I'd love to get a chance to read more religious texts and make a more educated decision on what it is I actually believe in.

Side note: Remember the story about always having your girl and play girl

I know I've always had an interest in Hinduism but never really taken a chance at finding a good book to teach myself. I'm pretty sure the Dharma (*this is wrong*) is their religious text and Shiva, Vishnu and Brahma are three of their main deities.

Come to find out one of the guys that I thought had been kicked from the unit is actually just a hermit at this point. He doesn't leave his room for pretty much any other reason than to get into fights with people. But I also found out my lunch buddies name. Quiet One.

Since sharing tonight, a lot of other people in the unit have actually started talking to me more. Which is honestly making me again feel so much more comfortable. I made a joke about how today may be the first day I've really talked, which was half a joke, but mostly the truth.

During group tonight one of my new roommates here in 'D' block shared a bit of a story about what he's been going through lately and why he hasn't been his usual self here lately. Since arriving I knew he had a visual impairment, but it's apparently getting worse. His biggest fear is that while he's here he'll fully lose his vision and never be able to see his wife or kid again. Whereas if he checks himself out now, he knows he'll go straight back to drinking. Either way it's a zero sum game.

One of the older black women of the group shared about how with aging and her addiction issues she has managed to go periods without using. But because she's aging she's getting more and more afraid of her kids getting "that" phone call.

Which also effected one of the other older women in the group "church lady". I found out that her addiction didn't start all that long ago and she actually went to a rehab about a year ago. Just six months ago she became a widow which I can only imagine didn't help her recovery process.

Overall today has been very productive in so many ways. Closer friendships (if that's what you call them), a clearer mind, another day sober, and finally finding my footing again with faith.

I had planned on reading some of the bible tonight, but it got late. Maybe in the morning?

7 — 12/11 - Sun.

Sunday is a very hard day as we went to Church. It was comforting as the whole church prayed for Zach. There are people from California - to NY - Florida - and Canada praying for Zach.

I know he will be okay. He is the first thing I think of in the morning and the last person on my mind and heart before I go to sleep. I love him so. I feel like I'm getting sick again.

People are calling in droves to see how he is. We all love him. Zach - get better honey.

12/14 – Weds.

I worked today, but my mind was not there. I pray for Zach daily and throughout the day. This AM I felt God's peace that Zach would be fine. I got a call later in the afternoon – Steph saying they were going to do surgery right away. Jim's in Syracuse, I called him and he said he would drive to Rochester.

[…]

I called him and he said he was there now. They took Zach at approximately 5:00 pm for surgery to his aorta valve. Ashley came over. She doesn't know what is going on as this would floor her. She has broke down several times tonight.

[…]

We prayed for Zach at approximately 8:45 pm. Jim called to say Zach was out of surgery and praise God he is fine. Thank you God for answered prayers. He may be coming home in four weeks or so.

8 – First Step, Fail

"Learning to walk in a tutorial is easy. Reteaching yourself to walk is hard."

When I got home, I faced a whole brand new set of struggles; with the help of a walker, I could move a little. I needed my mom for basic tasks, though. Early on, my mom figured out it was easiest just carrying me.

In my mind, the time had come to a standstill. Wrapping my head around everything that had happened with all of the medication I was on was impossible. I was operating, but something was tripping my understanding up.

TL groups, or Team Lead groups, were still around when I started Lambda. Initially, I was in a group with a female TL, Tiffany. We'd been introduced to the groups' idea during Orientation, but it was also kind of my first experience dealing with new people again.

While in rehab, they stress the importance of going to AA or NA meetings when you get out. With hard work and the right people in my corner, though, I'd decided Lambda School's schedule was more important for me.

I spent the first week with the same TL group, or at least until that Friday. After the coding sprint challenge, Tiffany let me know I was being switched. Mentally I wasn't prepared to reach out to these people I'd just started connecting to. At the same time, though, I could try again with my new TL group.

Some of my injuries had been immediately obvious to me. Some had to be explained. I now had two skin grafts and a burn on my forehead that turned a bright red. Any time I was emotional, it would become visible. The burns on my right knee left thigh, and abdomen had all been cut out and stitched back up.

No one's ever asked, but I'd have to say there's only one time I've had work done.

Every nurse I had was unbelievable. I'd been coughing a lot, and it was excruciating. So one of the nurses made me a cough pillow I could squeeze. Collapsed lungs and broken ribs make for poor bedfellows.

The brain bleeds healed, as well as the lacerated kidney, spleen, and liver.

I've only ever seen a local community do something so kind one other time. By this point, the local newspapers were running at least one story a day about my family. Sheltered from the actual news, stacks of cards and well wishes were coming in. There was just so much that it became a last in, first out kind of situation.

I'm not sure when exactly we received it but dated December 28, 2005, the day after I got discharged from the hospital, the letter said:

"Dear Parents of Zach Dunivan - Peterson:"

"Zach is invited to become a member of the Southern Tier area People to People Sports Ambassador Program delegation to Holland. As a member of the delegation, Zach will have the opportunity to improve as an athlete, compete Internationally in the Youth Friendship Games, and gain a better understanding of the world."

It continues to highlight all of the benefits of joining the program, and we even went to the initial meetings in the letter, planning on me being able to participate.

Right around the same time, though, my mom let me know that another organization would be dropping off whatever it was that I wanted. I could choose whatever, material or an experience; I decided on a GameCube and Pokemon XD.

When they came to deliver it, what the representative said is what stood out. He was from "Make A Wish." Having heaps of favorable treatment thrown my way, the rest of his words just went in and out. I'd already mentally prepared to die, so that fear was a non-issue. My concern was that it was already challenging to poop in privacy, but now I had to deal with cancer.

Thankfully, my mom noticed my expression and finally fully explained. The issue was with my heart and not cancer. What happened to me wasn't a brand new battle to fight, but a mini-win that I had no idea about beforehand.

Aortic dissection. More specifically, two of the three layers of my aorta had torn in the explosion- something generally reserved for adult patients, with the age group still trending older there.

80% mortality rate and that was without my other conditions.

Our house was right across the street from a Catholic School. Generally, after school, my sister and I would go there because they had an after school program. We weren't a part of it, but the playground was open.

On the playground was where I spent most of my days after school, but depending on the season, there was soccer practice too. When you're trying to plan things out while developing, combine them to display one thing in two ways, create a component.

Here I was, just across the street from one of my closest friends on my travel team. Heartbroken, wondering if I'd be able to play soccer and if any of my friendships would be the same. Was something I created now seemingly useless?

I decided that it was probably best not to start opening up with my new group. My new Team Lead's name was Aaron. One girl in our group whose vibe I liked, but it's not like I could just say that. Slack was a professional environment. Although I'm gay, it may not come off that way.

They don't tell you in rehab that those AA meetings are to help you get readjusted to interacting with people. People who've been there will have a lot better chance of understanding you. A lot of it is just syntax and framing.

When you stop giving people more experienced read access to your code, you make mistakes. Debugging is far more complicated, and you overlook logical errors.

Unit 2 of Lambda School was the hardest for me.

9 – Day Three: 7 Days Sober

CONTENT WARNING
Offensive Language

Today is just the day that keeps on giving. So far I've learned that it's possible to make a lighter out of staples. By hooking together the staples and attaching them to a battery you can light a cigarette. Which in turn has turned into a huge problem for the old room mate that fought the blind guy. The director is pretty much making rounds constantly now, and finding any and every possible hiding place.

While we were all sitting in the recreational room he came in and was inspecting all of the outlet cases in the room. Two of which he called to have screws placed in because you cold potentially remove them and place contraband in them.

Somehow all of the blow ups today brought us closer together, even making jokes about the situation like "code red, white and blue". Of all the things to bring people together this was probably the strangest.

Personally, I have no problem with counselor Big Guy. But apparently a majority of the guys in the block hate him. They've decided that because he's so hard on them it must be because he's looking at them in a sexual manner. Going as far as calling him a faggot and pretty much every other slur.

For me that's made things a little uncomfortable, but at the same time I've started to get comfortable with them after years of hearing it. At the same time though it does make me feel a little less comfortable about sharing certain things in the groups about my sexuality.

In the end, I'm sure I'll share it at some point. But I want to get more comfortable with the group before I actually open about that.

Complete juxtaposition, but had an amazing time at Yoga and realized that may be a really good way to de-stress. Albeit that calm was completely destroyed when Father Knowledge responded to my answer about my anger scale and how I sometimes fight with my mom.

"Any time you fight with your mom, that's a curse on you," he said.

"My relationship with my mom is between her and I," I not calmly responded.

Strangely enough the lesson tonight was supposed to be about anger management.

Different exercises to calm yourself down before you blow your top. Breathing exercises, muscle tension techniques, or like I'm doing now, writing your thoughts down so you can collect them.

Our speaker tonight for alcoholics anonymous reminded me a lot of my Grandfather. The speaker was an older gentleman that made a lot of jokes my grandfather would have. Also having the same taste in alcohol; any.

One of the strongest points he made was that for years he thought it was some kind of outside factor that was controlling his drinking; people, places, his job. But no matter who he met, where he went or the job he worked, the only definite thing he was bringing with him each time was himself.

I've heard that a million times, but again, just like the other day, for whatever reason hearing it from a stranger makes a greater impact.

Even with only being here for three days the emotional toll has been exhausting

Shame: I'm ashamed of a number of past decisions I've made. Obviously fighting with people, but also all of the times I've made a fool of myself doing things I really would have enjoyed more if I had been sober. Anzac day being a prime example. Being passed out on the lawn while a Prime Minister speaks is definitely not a good look, especially when even your friends are embarrassed to stand with you. I even tried cuddling with Jimmy that night.

Dishonesty: In so many ways I've been deceptive. There have definitely been a few times I've been outright dishonesty, but it's been very limited (probably being dishonest with myself here). Ever since dating He Who Shall Not Be Named I've gotten very good at telling half truths. Just enough of the truth to make it believable, but maybe with a few more of the interesting details than the boring ones. A lot of my lies have been in an effort to continue my drinking and keep people just far enough away that they wouldn't know how bad of a problem I had. I think a majority of the dishonesty has actually been with myself though.

Lack of Boundaries: The amount that I over extend myself because of saying yes when I should have said no is insane. Even before I started the recovery process I overshared things that should have stayed secret. Kept in confidence when I thought a person could fully be trusted, then just turned into ammo later.

Aggression/Passivity: With my bi-polar issues this is probably one of my worst issues. The definition of the obstacles of communication sums up my issues perfectly. Nine times out of ten I truly do leave conflicts unresolved, solely in the sense I leave the conflict open so if I need to take out anger, I'm free to at some point later.

10 – Game Over. Try Again?

> "We need never be ashamed of our tears."
> - Charles Dickens

A brute force approach to life has always been instinctual. By failing, you improve. Moving forward without understanding why just creating a longer process.

Initially learning to read, I had a similar approach. More information, more references. In second grade, I began reading Harry Potter. Something my teacher thought was out of a six or seven-year-old's grasp. When my teacher called my mom, my mom told her to quiz me. That was the end of that.

Had 2001 not been such a tough year for my family, I would have skipped third grade. Conceptualizing two-step word problems, numbers as words, twenty years later is still difficult. Honestly, that was probably for the best.

Physical learning is a lot different. A baby doesn't just decide it's going to walk. Brute force doesn't work as well when you're older. Sometimes struggling brings you down. Down to the actual ground.

Strong Memorial's doctors had lined up physical therapy, but I knew I was strong on my own. By the time someone told me your upper body was supposed to move when you're walking, I was already in High School.

Without initially being able to walk independently, school had come to me. Generally, when I'm focused on information, I've always gone to a private place. My bedroom in our house had a big closet right outside it, where my sister and I often played school. I can't remember who bought them, but we had a collection of encyclopedias in there.

My sister used to write in them all the time with a pen. It would make me so mad.

When things got stressful, it was a quick and easy escape. It would look like I was going to my bedroom, but I'd actually go in the closet and read. Occasionally peeking behind my mom's hanging coats like there was something on the other side. Sometimes even jokingly hiding behind them. Always hoping my mom or sister would come in so I could scare them.

My tutor was a familiar family friend. I was comfortable at home. I had favorable conditions to maximize my potential. When you're practicing for a game, though, you're supposed to keep the conditions close to real life.

When you build React applications, one of the biggest parts is building components. There are libraries, frameworks. You figure out the state of your data and develop your app based on all these conditions. Sometimes, the API you work with doesn't act exactly as expected, and changes have to be made.

By March, it looked like I was ready to go back to school. I still couldn't walk at 100%, though, so I couldn't take the stairs or participate in gym class. While on bed rest, I'd developed a bald spot, so they were going to let me wear a hat and gave me a copy of the school elevator key. I've never seen a Notre Dame Fighting Irish game, but they became my team.

At the end of each class, I'd have someone leave early with me and walk me to my next one.

Because I wasn't allowed in gym class, I had an extra study hall. I didn't really need either of the two. I already had so much free time. So I asked to start volunteering in the Library for one study hall. In my little sister Ashley's 5th-grade classroom for the other.

I was a boy who lived. So many things were just given to me. It's weird the first time someone asks you if you landed on the hood of a truck when the house exploded. That's what their parents had said.

Most people treated me like a porcelain doll. For the most part, the people who treated me as close to before the accident appreciated a little extra. I'm bald now, but my hair was significant to me back then. One day one of my classmates grabbed my hat in English class.

Still to this day, I remember Mr. Carpenter, my English teacher's look. It was sort of like something snapped in him, he didn't do anything crazy, but he went into a scary protective mode. Tall, angry, red.

Being embarrassed in front of the class isn't really that bad though.

Each unit at Lambda School is finished with a build week sprint. A team of people placed together to work on a single project. In my first unit, I had selected a sort of travel journal, but because it was mostly just HTML and CSS, I selected it again for the second unit. In 2019, I spent three months in New Zealand, and it has an exceptionally special place in my heart.

With that in mind, I went into the project super excited. Our first team meetings went great. Then when we actually started building, it was like there was nothing for us to do. We had a large team, six people, seven, including our project lead, project lead B.

At the same time, though, I had family visiting, and yes, I know Corona. But if we were visiting, there weren't many of us. Plus, I'd already had Corona months before, and now I was spending all of my time inside with school.

I would only visit with them in the evenings, though, and that Tuesday was the first time I missed an evening stand up.

On Wednesday morning, when I went to look at our code, the footer I'd been working on had been deleted. It was merged to the main branch and then deleted from it. I had noticed something off with my code the night before and talked with the other React 1 dev and my Team Lead A. She also said there were some issues with hers.

Initially, I wasn't going to say anything. But when I saw that it had actually been deleted after the changes, I was pissed. Nobody knew I was struggling. The only reason I still had the footer file on my computer was that it was in a backup folder I had forgotten to delete the day before. My flow was all sorts of off.

In a recovering alcoholic fashion, I tried to express my concerns. But everything came out all wrong and definitely over the top compared to how I really felt.

Unfortunately, when you set far too high expectations for yourself and can't express what's going on to others in a meaningful way, you set yourself up to idle in the background while your inner daemon operates.

Sometimes all you need to do is open up—just a bit.

11 — Day Four: 8 Days Sober

CONTENT WARNING
Offensive language

Last night I had the strangest/worst nightmare. I can't really remember what exactly it was about I just remember waking up a few times last night and then this morning knowing it was weird. Not drinking as much has definitely brought up a lot of memories of different stressful times in my life.

Breakfast was fairly easy again this morning, no drama. Spirituality starts again here shortly and I start my new medicines that are three times a day.

"This will balance the beam between your alcohol dependence and need for feeling numb," my psychiatrist described it.

It shouldn't be surprising, but there are actually people here I have more in common with than I thought. People that have also been through traumatic experiences that have brought them close/near to death. There's also a lot more people with PTSD here that I ever would have originally imagined.

"Uncomfortability is a catalyst for change," I can still hear Mrs. Rose saying as she closed spirituality.

Which in some ways was a sign of things to come. Right after spirituality Willie gave me the folder so from now on I'll be running the 'D' wing spirituality and introductions. With the limited number of guys we have it's going to be difficult to find speakers, so I know I'll unfortunately be sharing a lot of stories and pretty much laying my soul bare.

Strangely though, I'm kind of excited for it. When Mrs. Rose shared the quote for whatever reason it was inspiring to me. So now I'll be stepping out of my comfort zone and exploring my faith and spirituality at the same time.

Currently I'm thinking of coming up with some sort of analogy on how sometimes we all get lost, and that's okay. We don't always follow the same path but when we realize we're going in the wrong direction it's time to turn around. You never know what's around the next bend, and the sooner you make the decision to walk the right path the better.

We've been focusing on communication in our group sessions, which was just random, but the entire day has been kind of suited for it. Our entire activity was one listener and one speaker, and the listener couldn't say anything to the speaker. The entire point of the exercise was to recreate the image the speaker saw with just explaining what you saw.

Lady Gray and I's image looked nothing like the picture I saw (I was speaker)

After the exercise was over we had to explain our experience and the difficulties we had as we were going through. I realized that the way I was describing things was very linear, kind of like reading a book. From top to bottom, from left to right. So at a lot of times I dropped necessary words like from left to right because in my mind that was just how I thought she would interpret it.

Lady Gray followed a lot of my directions, but because of my lack of where to place the shapes all of them were there; just jumbled up in ways that could have easily been fixed if I had been more concise with my directions.

Right off the bat I realized that the exercise was a lot like traveling and moving to different places. Practically all of the words (minus slang) are the same, but the context of them may be taken so completely different.

When I was in New Zealand and Phil from the UK would say he was going to smoke a "fag". Clearly it's not too difficult to tell that I'm gay, but in that moment I didn't react what so ever because I wasn't sure how people would respond especially straight guys from different countries.

Coming down to an actual context though it's very easy to just get stuck in a certain form of communication and not think of the other persons perspective.

Our counselor today gave a great example of when someone is trying to tell you a story of something they saw or did. To them certain moments stand out because they considered them to be the most important. Other details either not being brought up or not even noticed in the first place. Whereas if the person listening to the story had been in the same situation, the retelling would be so vastly different.

Not because the two people experienced different events, but because what they took from the experience was different. One of Mrs. Rose's phrases that I've heard so far was take the cotton out of your ears and put it in your mouth. Which for me can be extremely easy, or extremely difficult. Completely depending on time, place, who I'm dealing with, and especially my level of sobriety at the given time.

Certain instances I can't keep my mouth shut, other times I can't stop talking. A negative trait that I shared in group with Big Guy today. In more than one aspect of my life where I thought I was extremely good or at least better than most, I'm actually lacking.

There was only a little bit of time between the group meeting and the meeting with our case managers. I did however manage to fit in some time with my case manager S before the group meeting started and finally was able to get a hold of my mom.

My mom should be sending a package out tomorrow with a pair of pants, a new pair of sweats, and a pair of shoes. I completely forgot about asking her to put money into my account for the gift shop, which I think is just a really nice name for commissary.

Because of the limited time you can spend on the phone in the counselors office it's been almost a week since I've been able to talk to my Grandma Savino and even longer since I've been able to talk to a lot of the other people I'm so used to speaking to daily.

Over the next few days I'm going to try my best to kind of monitor my medicine's because I still have been having cravings. Depending on the results, I'm thinking about getting the vivitrol shot; which if I do, I'll not be able to drink for at least a month. If I continue to get the shot monthly, like I'm supposed to do, I won't be able to drink at all.

In the end that is the ultimate goal, but the idea of never being able to drink again is for whatever reason extremely intimidating and in a few ways terrifying to me.

Although my case manager S doesn't seem like the most pleasant person in the world, during our case management session she did give us a few ways to refocus our attention and relax. Between breathing and focusing on specific things and listing different breeds of dogs or some sort of category that you can just keep listing off.

While we did our mediation and breathing tonight the first thing I focused on was the different beaches, lakes and scenery in New Zealand. Focusing on Franz Josef and skydiving from 18,000 feet there. Seeing the glacier (possibly for the first and last time), the beach and ocean, as well as the huge forest.

Getting and staying sober may very well be the chance I need to actually get back to where I want to be; back in Auckland with my New Zealand family.

I know at first going there and staying sober would be a challenge, but I also know that with the right support system there I would be able to.

As to regards of the case manager meeting, I truly believe that meditation and yoga may be getting introduced into my weekly routine.

Meditation probably daily for at least a little while, even if it is only for a few minutes, it's progress. Yoga on Monday's and Friday's while I'm in here, however long that may be.

Actually that's been quite aggravating considering pretty much everyone else here has been given a tentative date. A lot of release dates have been changing for people, and yes, that does make it feel even more like a prison.

"I just want someone who represents us."

"I just want someone who represents us."

"I just want someone who represents us."

I've been replaying those words in my head for the past few hours. I won't be leading spirituality for 'D' block because The Leader has decided he wants to do it (although he's only been to one).

His reasoning for wanting to do it? Yep. "I just want someone who represents us."

I've chosen to take that as someone from the city. Having already wanted to leave since day one because I didn't feel like I fit in and then actually hearing someone vocalize it makes perfect sense for a place to seek recovery for damage done, right.

Everyone else kind of came to my defense and said that I was a part of the group and that I was one of them, but I already know in the back of their minds a majority of them agreed.

The only people I've really had any interaction with since I've been here are the other people that have kind of been cast to the side, and a few of the girls.

Thinking the fact I was gay was hidden even temporarily might as well have been a pipe dream. Because The Leader doesn't like me for some reason and I know for a fact it's not because he's gotten to know me.

Really the only solace here is that The Leader doesn't wake up in time for breakfast a majority of the time. So the chances of him making it to spirituality are slim to none. And I know I shouldn't think this way, but I actually really enjoy spirituality and I know he won't be there to ruin it.

Beyond that, the only person he's going to be embarrassing is himself. The three people that do regularly show up will still be there for as long as we're in the building.

What bothers me the most though is that there are so many people here who are absolutely squandering this opportunity. It took me about two weeks to find a bed three and a half hours away minimum. There will be no chance to visit with my family because the facility requires them to be here all day to participate, and family day starts at 9:30 am. which would mean leaving by 5:00 am. to afford time for traffic and tolls; even earlier if my grandma and Ashley wanted to come.

A lot of people here are mandated by law, so I understand why they might not want to be here. The far and few in between that are here voluntarily are getting the short end of the stick. Majority of the groups the people talking the most are the ones who want to be here the least.

All of this was really just meant to lead up to the part where I explained how I now once again feel uncomfortable in my wing and I was seeing red through the last two meetings of the day so I barely remember a thing they said. The Leader has the folder now, so I guess we'll just see how things go.

12 — 1,000 words.

CONTENT WARNING
Graphic Content

People learn things in such a subjective way. Now and then, when you try something new, it just clicks with you. Stuff you were struggling with become crystal clear. Someone there to help you along the way, even better.

That was Unit three for me. Our instructor recommended hand drawing diagrams when you're planning things out. You can see where things will be going and move them around a little more comfortably in your mind.

At the same time, I had started sending messages to the developer I had just finished working with the previous build week. We had hit it off, despite all the drama I caused.

Seventh grade is a lot different. My schedule was like everyone else, except for gym swapped with study halls.

I've never been good at science. Terrible actually. Always my worst subject and far too research-based for me. History was facts, and those can't change. Just the way people portray them.

Logic came later for me in life—practically a language of its own.

Often, I'd zone out in Mr. Hartman's class. Science words had that effect. Our desks were tables, sitting side by side. I sat next to someone I was friendly with from skiing the years before my accident.

We would get lost in the woods, which was super against the rules. But pre-teen years, rules are meant to be broken. There were bus trips up to Greek Peak on the weekend and people I, for the most part, have in my life still today.

This particular day though, I happened to glance over, and he was drawing. At first, I didn't pay any attention, but I saw my name as I was looking away.

Next to an exploding house.

Up in the sky.

A little stick body.

Zach Peterson

13 — Day Five: 9 Days Sober

CONTENT WARNING
Offensive Language

It took The Leader one night, one night to leave the spirituality notes out, and I was also booted from the job of doing coffee at some point. But then volun-told this morning because I was more consistent I should be in charge. Hmm?

Honestly this place is run like a prison, people talking about getting single cigarettes from different blocks for $5. The entire situation is just bullshit.

After breakfast this morning I came back into the lounge/rec room and cleaned up. All of which went to shit really quickly and now the spirituality notes and folder are missing. Thankfully tomorrow morning for spirituality it's a special event with alumni that have been out for ninety-days and gone to ninety-days worth of meetings.

Our first group of the day was our block spirituality, we read from "Desiderata", which our counselor had no clue what it meant. But it had a lot of reaffirming statements close to the book of Psalms in the Bible. We also read from the book "365 Zen", which follows more of Buddhist principles. The major gain from the group was that we all want to be unique but at the same time we're all still interconnected in so many ways.

After group I checked in with my case manager and got my "release date" which isn't until March 20th. Which very well could be moved later, but will give me a total of thirty-three days in sober living.

Hopefully that will be enough, but until then I'll just continue with groups and taking things day by day. Movie Star found out today that she won't be able to get into outpatient, so she's upset. She thinks that will be the big drama today, but I have a feeling more is to come.

So far so good, and that's after two more meetings. Our milieu group as well as our case manager rules/community meeting. Which the case manager meeting doesn't really make sense to me, because the newest person wasn't even there.

Even stranger than though, I found out that the 'D' block is actually an experimental unit and the first of it's kind here at Arms Acres. So in some sense we're testing out the possibility of setting up co-ed wings here in the future.

Personally I don't know how well that would work, but seeing that half the unit is leaving within the next week or two I'll get to experience a fresh batch of both guys and girls. Our personalities may get a long wonderfully, or there could be clashes. Who knows.

Either way it makes you wonder what buttons the staff are trying to push to see our reactions; especially given that counselor Big Guy read from, or described really, an experiment about rats given water or water with morphine in a metal cage, basically no necessities. The rats all became addicted to morphine.

Another experiment places the rats in a cage with all of the necessities as well as other rats with both the normal water and water with morphine. All of the rats stayed clean.

In fact, when the addicted rats were introduced they even became clean. Ultimately an analogy about how when you have what you need it's not only easier to avoid addiction, but possible to find a way back from it.

Our main group this morning was about sleep patterns and different types of insomnia. Nurse P, our unit's main nurse, pretty much covered basic knowledge and gave us some tips on how to have a deeper sleep. Avoiding light, caffeine after 6:00 pm. and mainly using your bed for sleep.

A lot of it was common knowledge. But still useful to hear out loud.

Going back to the meeting with our case managers, don't worry this is going somewhere, Usual Suspect made a comment about how there are no snitches in this group.

Flash forward to tonight's AA meeting, I'm living with some of the most disrespectful men I've ever met. Not only were drug deals going on "secretly" during the meeting, people were having background conversations so loud it was hard to hear the speaker talk about his brother he watched die at age five, or his daughter that died in the hospital at the age of fourteen; pretty much the entire story of how he became an alcoholic and got to the place he's at in life now. Father Knowledge was so rude as to make a joke as the speaker spoke about a man that practically saved his life that he watched die.

Every day that passes I realize more and more that this facility is like a real life episode of 'Orange Is The New Black.' People's stuff being stolen left and right, passing notes (most likely to schedule drug deliveries), literal hand offs and make shift lighters to smoke a little bit of pocket tobacco wrapped in toilet paper during night shift, even cooking left over food on the coffee machine that they stole from the mess hall.

I truly hope there is no next time, and partially the reason why I'm keeping this journal. A reminder of all of the negative things that happened and how shitty they could be. Honestly I can't wait to compare stories with Ashley, because I guarantee I'm having a far different experience than she did.

There's practically a gang forming in my unit that's now known for selling cigarettes to other units with one of the main runners literally being a cocaine dealer on the outside whose addiction is to hustling; reminding everyone that there are no snitches in this group.

Thankfully I saw no fights today, but then again tomorrow is a new day and a new roommate. Since Mr. Willie moved in, this room has been quiet. Mr. Charles, Mr. Willie and I have gotten along so well.

Quiet One, the guy I eat meals with (who has also started opening up and talking to me more), got a new roommate today from detox and within the first few hours of him being here got accused of stealing the new guys bracelet. Which was then found only like two minutes later.

With Mr. Willie leaving, I'll have had six roommates in my first six days. By the time I'm finished here I'll have certainly surpassed the number of roommates I had at Las Palmas, and I lived there for three years.

On a brighter note though, I finally got my first mail. Grandma Savino sent her first card, and included a few pictures to pick up my spirits (pun intended). My mom should hopefully have gotten out my clothes and shoes package today, so I should be receiving that in the next day or two hopefully, all really depends on the form of shipping she chose.

The AA speaker tonight again really reminded me of my Grandpa Tom. Irish to the tee and made just as crazy of jokes with lots of trauma in life. I know he's out there somewhere looking over me; but most of all I hope he's proud and knows that I keep Bonus Mom and the girls in my thoughts.

I'm going to possibly read a passage or two of my Bible and then meditate for a bit before bed.

Praying for as calm of a day tomorrow as the one we had today.

14 − next()

> "I avoid looking forward or backward, and try to keep looking upward."
> - Charlotte Brontë

Freshman and Sophomore year of high school were formative, I learned that in the end I had to be myself. It wasn't enough for me to just do one thing, it was a complex intermingling of pieces within myself. I wanted to be involved in everything that I could, controlling my own path forward in a way. I never set out to make an impact in any of the organizations, but through my experiences with them, other leaders made impressions that impact decisions I still make to this day.

By the end of Sophomore year, I had easily spent another 30 days in the hospital. My body wasn't able to keep up with everything that I was trying to do, and my blood pressure was rising to heights like 170/85 while resting.

In algebra one day, I raised my hand to go to the nurse, I would get pounding migraines over my left eye. I don't even remember how long my hand was raised, I just asked, "May I go to the nurse?"

Mr. R replied "Of course."

As I stood up, the ground came rushing forward. Initially, you think it's yourself waking up from a nightmare. Falling towards the ground.

Helping me up Mr. R asked, "Are you okay?" The nurse had assembled and an ambulance was on it's way.

Rushing me off to the hospital, they made sure to let my parents, as well as my grandparents, who were my immediate emergency contacts, know where I was headed. Initially running the full gambit of tests I had grown accustomed to.

First up, EKG stickies getting gunk on every possible limb, as well as covering your torso. Next up was a CT with contrast, the tiny tunnel of doom that makes you feel as if you need to pee. Followed up and finished by an X-ray of the chest to double check that I hadn't broken any ribs. The tests showed nothing.

They released me that night with inconclusive results, suggesting possible muscle spasms and a hot compress to relax the muscles whenever they would tense up. Getting home I laid down and just wanted to get some rest. After being in the hospital I normally closed off from the world, even if it was only a brief stay.

My father still lived out of town, but had driven in when he had gotten the call to make sure that I was okay, so we were all staying at my grandparents. Walking to the kitchen to grab a snack I reached up for a box of crackers.

"Zach are you okay?"

This time I didn't recognize all of the faces around me. My father, and grandparents were there, but so were a bunch of others. The ambulance had already arrived, and one of the paramedics had used their knuckle to wake me up.

Groggy once again, I asked "What's going on?"

This time at the hospital we skipped the initial tests, and I was transported to a floor instead of an emergency room. The doctors would make their rounds in the morning, but for the night I had to be monitored.

By morning I was ready to go. I'd learned to understand vital signs in the most basic of forms, so I knew everyone would be happy with what I'd seen the previous night, forgetting about both spells of passing out.

To my surprise the doctors ordered an additional test. One I'd never had at Arnot before that. A special test, meant to look at the pressure through ultrasounds. My mind immediately went to babies, and moms of newborns.

At the time, I didn't put it all together. But now that I look back, I've noticed a pattern.

When things would get stressful, I'd throw myself into whatever I was doing. Forgetting my hierarchy of needs is common. One of the few times I went skiing after my accident, I ended up in the hospital, my blood pressure once again too high. Systolic close to 200.

All I knew was that whatever they'd found on the ultrasound had changed the way the doctors were looking at my case, now I was being sent to a different hospital by plane.

Cleveland Clinic was a different style hospital than I was used to. When we landed I went through the checklist, but instead of a private room, I was put into a pod. Basically a room shared with five beds and each has a privacy screen in between.

After they ran some more tests is when they found the issue. When I'd raised my hand in class that day, the placement of the stint somehow cut off blood flow to my brain. So when I stood up, I fell down. The homeostasis of my aortic blood pressure was off because of the placement.

While in Cleveland, my best friend came to visit. She'd started making appearances anytime I was in the hospital, just as I had started doing for her. As an asthmatic she had spent sometime in ICU's as well.

Keeping me company we would make jokes about things like my dad snoring, or the one time that she'd stayed up at my house in Brockport and thought it was a ghost in the house. Anything to keep my mind off of the up coming surgery.

When the doctors found out that back at home, the youth bureau was shipping up to start the event of the year, the youth bureau lock in, they even let me go. My surgery wasn't scheduled until the following week, so I got a weekend pass to participate. Leading a home/family group influencing a lot of my leadership decision making still now.

After the event it was straight back to the hospital, as it was I didn't make it through the entire lock-in; falling asleep mid-way through on the auditorium floor.

15 — Day Six: 10 Days Sober

"Experience is not what happens to you, it is what you do with what happens to you."
- Aldous Huxley

As small as it sounds, getting to watch the morning news and having a cup of coffee are quickly becoming one of my favorite parts of the day.

Everything happening outside the facility is a little crazy, but just knowing is nice. You get a little stuck in the rehab mentality and it's almost as if you know nothing about what's going on on the outside.

No big surprise, but The Leader of course didn't end up going to spirituality, and even though we are doing Alco-thon today we ended up needing to do the mantra and share. There were five of us instead of the three last time. Sure enough the first person to share from 'A' block brought up the fact that the guys in our group were selling cigarettes. He didn't pinpoint our group specifically, but I do know he was because I've already seen first hand and heard them talk about it.

Because a majority of the guys in our unit barely show up (and the ones who do don't want to speak, I ended up being the one to speak for 'D' wing again. I spoke sort of a variation of what I had panned on saying originally, but having to improv on the spot kind of tripped me up.

This time though, I was a little more confident and my nerves weren't nearly as bad. Instead of just standing in one place looking forward, this time, I was able to move and look around a bit more.

If this sequence is any sign of what's to come I'll probably be speaking a lot more over the next few weeks at spirituality, and I wouldn't be surprised if eventually I am the group leader.

A lot of the people in the 'D' block don't really care about how things are run around here or if things are kept clean and stocked up, its pretty much a dog eat dog world in here.

Because it's Alco-thon we had two guest speakers come in instead of our usual Milieu group meeting. The unit has been losing people that just keep getting replaced like crazy. During the two guest speakers I noticed Angry One but really didn't think much of it because he rarely shows up to the meetings anyway. Sure enough he got into it with the counselors again and got kicked out of the program.

Our two speakers were absolutely amazing though. The first gentleman was an older guy that if you saw him on the street you'd picture your grandfather, the kind of guy you'd never imagine having more than a glass of scotch or whiskey with a cigar after dinner.

When he first began to speak you could tell he had an accent. But what he was saying was far from what you would associate with the way he looks now. Kind of a friendly reminder not to judge a book by its cover.

It's hard when strangers tell stories about their past, because you can really only picture them the way that they look now; and this little old man from Norway telling a story about getting robbed at knife point for the twenty dollars in his back pocket was pretty hard to picture.

"I didn't really care though because I had fifty dollars in my sock. Addicts are clever," he said.

Our second speaker hadn't arrived at this point, so we kind of just went into a group discussion. One where again a number of people expressed how sick of being here they are. They brought up how things have gotten repetitive, which they have, but at the same time acknowledged that repetition is one of the best ways to learn. In some ways a bit of a paradox.

A lot of the people that you don't normally hear from did speak. Young-One even shared about losing her child's father to an overdose, and as she put it, how it should have been a wake up call.

"I just used it as another reason to get high," she said.

It was an instant flashback to when my mom ended up in the hospital when I was in LA and only Ashley was there with her to get help. I got the call that it was touch and go as to whether my mom was going to survive. Instead of that being a wake up call for me I got extremely drunk that day, and because of the time change started at 11:00 am.

When our second speaker shower up we were in the middle of our discussion, so in the end we only got to hear him share his story and not really talk with him. He was as well a well put together gentleman, but from what he was saying a little over eleven years ago, while he was still in active addiction, there would be times he would tell his wife he was going to the store for something and show back up four weeks later with the same clothes on just coming off a month long bender.

He shared that when he left the bar, he would find himself in abandoned houses where the windows were boarded up, looking through the cracks to see if anyone was coming while he smoked.

Now though, after eleven and a half years sober, he's been with his wife (who never left him) and has a son who is eight years old and never seen him in active addiction.

Honestly both stories were very inspiring only to be followed by a crazy afternoon of more arguing and more problems between the guys (the three) and Big Guy. They're now writing letters complaining about how Big Guy acts towards them specifically.

Personally, I've had no issues with any of the counselors, but that's again a perk of me being quiet. So far that hasn't been to big of a blow up yet, just some arguing about what they should do and how to write a letter to the supervisor to complain about him. Jelly-Belly pretty much said that the only thing that would happen would be the three of them getting moved to different units themselves.

After all this drama kind of happened we got another speaker for Alco-thon. His name was X and he was decked to the tee in Yankees.

He kept hitting on this point, "Do you want to live, or do you want to die?"

Every time he made a deep statement or told a story he would repeat that phrase.

We got our new roommate, his name is the Giant. So far he seems like a really nice guy and quiet, but you can tell he's still detoxing at the same time. It'll be a few days before we probably get to see his actual personality. Either way though, he's practically a giant, seems to be in good shape and has a blonde mow hawk.

Drug of choice seems to actually be a phrase people ask here.

"Drug of choice," Jelly-Belly asked?

"I'm a drinker. Alcohol," I admitted inquisitively.

"You never know, I've heard floor cleaner before," she said.

Rehab in general is weird.

Fairly certain that there won't be a day here without some type of fight. At this point it just seems like living in a house with an abusive partner, constant yelling and screaming, the constant threat of physical violence and the smallest thing sets people off and them reacting above and beyond what a normal person should respond like.

Our case manager meeting tonight was with someone I hadn't met before. His whole meeting was about the boogie man in the closet. Which in the end was an analogy about us and our addiction, and "how to bring the boogie man out of the closet".

16 – Free Falling

> "O death, where is your victory? O death, where is your sting?"
> -Corinthians 15:55

There truly is nothing quite like jumping from 18,000 feet in the sky that gets you questioning your mortality. Philosophy 101 our professor introduced himself, and then went into a story about how he lived a life full of sex, drugs and rock and roll before becoming a professor. His teachings of ethics, faith and logic still influence my life to this day.

While in New Zealand, I jumped out of a plane five times across both North and South Island. My favorite being at Franz Glacier, possibly my first and last there with such a view. Circling through the sky, instructor attached, I learned about the rigging after directing us through the sky, practicing my canopying skills.

A panorama view, 360 degree circles, snow capped-glacier, a never-ending forest, then the ocean rolling ashore. Three entirely different worlds, me choosing which glimpse we would get next.

For whatever reason I'm never afraid of the jump or fall, only the plane ride up. Yet every time I board a plane the take off and landing raise my anxiety to a fever pitch. On a rickety plane this fear makes sense, but an irrational one I have no matter the planes make.

Falling through clouds though, you truly feel free. A certain sense of calmness even should you hypothetically be falling towards your death. What lasts minutes feels as if a lifetime in the sky.

As your toes touch the edge of the door, your stomach somersaults jumping from the side of the plane, gravity takes affect and you're free falling.

New Zealand wasn't all fun though, in Christchurch I don't even have the words to explain what happened. The walls went up in my head as soon as the bar got locked down inside.

I couldn't go back to my hostel, as a mass shooter was at large. The bartender Zach's mom working out opposite the YMCA's sleeping quarters. She too unable to move.

A sense of fear should have settled, but instead I was empty, nothing inside. One of my least intoxicated days on holiday before the events began unfolding. Everything was happening so quickly, yet not at all.

A paradox of sorts, the rapid fire of information not connecting, missing its mark. Of all the times to be afraid this was the one.

After a few hours passed we were still stuck inside. News of death and mayhem right outside the door, the staff was figuring out how to keep us comfortable at what should have been a time of distress. Yet all I could do was order another round of coronas.

Safety declared, we'd been in the middle of the two attack sites. My hostel, Zach's mom, just across the park from where the first rounds were fired. Still now I've not let myself feel or that day. Dropping off flowers and visiting local vigils, I experienced how close tragedy can bring a united nation. There was no time for division in the midst of distress.

I extended my stay, going back to Terrace Tavern everyday. Making myself so ingratiated they even offered me a job. In that moment, all of my plans changed and I booked a flight. I was going to Auckland.

"I'll be back in a night," I told everyone, "I just need to go to the embassy and renew my passport."

17 – Enter Stage Left

> "...but simply recall that it is through sin that one first catches sight of salvation."
> -Soren Kierkegaard

After my second heart surgery, I ended up deciding that there was a lot I wanted to leave behind in Elmira. That it was time to move back in with my dad. So heading into Junior year, everything changed. I was going back to a school where I didn't really know anyone, and in Brockport I hadn't really found any extra-curricular activities.

We lived next door to one of our school district's health teachers, who also directed the middle school theater productions. Having arrived back in Brockport the summer before, he was able to get me a spot in the high school musical "Thoroughly Modern Millie".

I wasn't super talented when it came to music. Singing a solo from the Phantom of the Opera in 5th grade, and performing in one other musical in intermediate school, but that was the extent of my musical experience. I played trumpet for about a year, but I could never really get into practicing. I did however get to put my new dance skills to the test, completely screwing up the tap solo at one of our performances.

I also auditioned for mad vocals, a jazz ensemble that also sang accapella. I found out about the audition the day of and learned "Seasons of Love" from Rent to sing for the audition that afternoon. I was one of the 3 bass singers selected in the twenty member group.

Other than the musical, and mad vocals it was strictly dance.

I had begun dancing at a more advanced level, but still with kids much younger than me. So on top of the normal classes I also took formal ballet private lessons. As well as modern private lessons to start working on a routine for auditioning.

Collectively taking ballet, modern, tap and jazz.

This is when I began making a solid group of friends, and where the nickname Zip comes from. "Thoroughly Modern Millie" was pretty much an introduction into getting to finally fully be myself.

Now that I had come out, and everyone knew a majority of my life story there was nothing to stop me from just being. I was at times over the top, but that came with being a part of the theater crowd. Certain things I still liked to keep at least semi-private.

Gym classes were never really the same after my accident. Other than Sophomore year when an old team mate and I were put on a team playing soccer together, nicknamed thunder and lightning for our performance on the field, I was mostly designated to the library to write book reports.

Brockport gym classes I still had to sit out of anything that was considered too high of a risk. So I went inline skating, and did things like self defense classes. My all time favorite though was bowling. More specifically, street bowling. Bowling at the bowling alley was just a quick drive from the high school, our initials on the lane scoreboard spelled out JEDZ which became a whole thing for a bit.

Anything we were assigned in gym could become a street game, JEDZ just needed to get their hands on it. It was simple. Whatever the rules were, you just add some more as you go. Badminton became street badminton by having to hit the birdie an extra couple of times when it was on your side of the net. Or for golf to become street golf you would just have to spin in a circle with your nose on the club three times before you could try to hit the ball.

Honestly, I have no clue how we got away with a lot of the stuff that we did in class. But Gym teachers and English teachers always seemed to love me.

Second semester of Junior year, I did the school play. Where I met probably the most influential person in my life from high school that I can think of. Mr. Izzo.

I don't know what it was about Mr. Izzo, I don't think I even talked to him that much when we first met. But he has this unbelievably inspiring presence. One of those people you meet and know is brilliant. One of his daughters made up the D in JEDZ, so that probably also helped.

Finally I was connecting with real people that I shared a common bond with. All while figuring out exactly what it was that I needed to do to focus.

Senior year was a completely different beast. Practically everyone I knew graduated. So going in, I felt more comfortable but again a little alone. The feeling didn't last long though, because a lot of the connections I'd made, but not fostered, grew stronger. Building the relationships up took a bit of effort, but in the end sometimes even with different paths, you still end up in the same place mentally.

At a young age I had gotten ahead. Talk at one point when in 6th grade led to taking advanced classes, later. By Junior year, I had already finished all of my core math classes as well as five years worth of French. So, I had a lot of empty room in my schedule both Junior and Senior year.

Brockport had gotten rid of early release and late arrival, so my schedule was filled with a bunch of extra-curricular activities. Junior year, I took Sculpture, Photography, and even managed to squeeze in an impromptu study hall during what our normal advisement time was.

By Senior year, I was finished with all of my core classes except for English and Science. I started taking AP economics and AP government so that I could get ahead for college. One thing I did not do though, was take a single AP test, and my reasoning was simple.

Take the AP classes once, and not test on them. Then when I got to college I could take my intro courses, and I'd be able to kind of skate through my classes because I'd already have a general idea of the information I needed to know.

A longer process, but one that ensured I retained the most information.

Sociology, Public Speaking, Improvisation, a level-two photography class. I had a lot of free periods Senior year. With Advisement even turning into a hangout for me in Mrs. Contrera's classroom. One steady perk though, was that everyday I had class with Mr. Izzo. My favorite teacher.

Imrpov. AP English.

A Day. B Day.

Public Speaking, AP English.

A Day. B Day.

Mr Izzo teaching about life in them all. One of our assigned readings was Grendel.

Senior year I read a lot of books and wrote a lot of essays. Even writing an essay in Mrs. Contrera's hangout room on Harvey Milk, a leader in Political Courage. I still made a lot of mistakes though. It's only important to note because somehow when I wrote my paper on Grendel, I managed to spell Grendel Grendle. Every. Single. Time.

Working through existentialism and nihilism at 17 years old is strange. We live in a time now where life has been advanced so greatly by society that it's strange for tribal traditions from the time of Beowulf to be inspiring ideas, but you can find magic anywhere.

Using my own life and experiences as a lens, I was also able to help out my friend, and Mrs. Contrera's daughter, with a passion project she started. Keep The Peace. We had danced together the year before so it was one of those connections I just needed to foster more attentively.

I consider myself a co-founder in the sense that Stephanie had the idea for the club, a majority of what it's purpose was, and had done a majority of the leg work to get the school on board. When I came to the project, all that was missing was the actual event that tied it all together.

This was my first experience with event planning, but I had some background from the Youth Bureau lock-in. An event focused on keeping youth on a straight and narrow track. No drugs. No alcohol.

Keep the Peace was tasked with a half school day event. We just needed to fill up the time slots. We originally were shooting for a full day, but I was the only one in Brockport who had experienced the lock-in, so a lot of training fell back on me.

We used a family group model, directly in our advisement rooms. During the half day we did ice breaker activities, and at one point had the entire student body fill the halls to do a crossing the line activity.

If you'd experienced harassment, abuse, any sort of trauma big or small you could watch down the hallway to know you were not alone. There's strength in numbers, even if they're just in your head. That memory sits with me today.

I am not alone.

You are not alone.

We are stronger together.

18 – Sweet as

> "For before this I was born once a boy, and a maiden, and a plant, and a bird, and a darting fish in the sea."
> - Empedocles

While I was traveling with the Kiwi experience, we mostly stayed in hostels. On rare occasion, we could get a special bunking arrangement where we all shared a cabin, but for the most part, it was small rooms with a lot of people.

After skydiving in Franz Josef, I arrived in Queenstown for my first time. Pub Crawl on the very first night, I was singing and having a grand time by the end of the evening. I met a guy moving to Ireland, and a bar filled with employees from Syracuse, New York. Queenstown started to feel a lot like home. My first night in the hostel there was a bed bug scare, my hostel room got moved, and they offered free dry cleaning.

I only spent two nights there my first time through. I had the add on package to do the deep south, so there was an extra loop back through after Dunedin and Invercargill. The Deep South of New Zealand is exactly what it sounds like. There wasn't a whole lot of anything. I did meet some pretty cool people though, special thanks to Specks and D-Rock for sharing some drinks that lonely night in Invercargill.

Getting back into Queenstown was a long ride, solely because of the Milford Sound excursion, my first experience with a fjord. All in all, a lot of water.

Arriving back into Queenstown is when I finally ran back into the powderpuff girls. Dee, Tee, and Lee. Dee being my favorite. All three are from Canada. All three making Queenstown even more fun than the first time through. Again with a pub crawl on the very first night.

This pub crawl was extra special, though, because it included games and prizes. A potato between the legs squat walk, a karaoke contest, and some limbo variation. Our group won them all, but Dee was pretty sure it was because our tour guide had a crush on me.

In Queenstown, the clubs stay open late on the weekends, the pub crawl itself not even ending until 1:00 am. We had two hours left in them before the closing call. Queenstown is built in a grid-like fashion, and all of the best places for people backpacking tend to be grouped, so we just kept hitting other spots.

Being intoxicated with cool people makes you never want to stop that night, so I ended up booking us hotel rooms close to the bar so we could get a good nights sleep.

The next day I woke up with a wicked hangover, but I was going bungee jumping. The Nevis, the biggest in New Zealand, and has a tiny little cabin-like structure hanging in the middle of a canyon. Oh, it also has a glass floor. So to prepare myself, I drank three corona's and threw on the sweats and t-shirt from inside my backpack that normally acted as a cooler for any contraband beer I may have in the hostel.

For whatever reason, potentially jumping to my death thrilled me so much, I ended up doing the slingshot, making friends with some people who ended up taking pictures of me along the way.

19 — Day Seven: 11 Days Sober

> "Everyone thinks of changing the world, but no one thinks of changing himself."
> - Leo Tolstoy

I never really finished yesterday's meetings and writing them down/describing them. After the case manager meeting we had a small break and then had our last AA meeting for the night.

Other than being distracted by the guys that did come to the meeting, it was overall a pretty good one. When it's just the guys in the meetings the speakers tend to be a little more candid.

Our speaker was the typical biker and had started drinking at a young age quickly followed up by drug use. He started in motocross at a fairly young age and went to the race circuits mostly for the parties afterwards. His reason for being there was to race, but he kept going because of the parties.

Now that he's older and he's been in long term sobriety he's managed to place and win some races.

This mornings meeting was a co-occurring dependence meeting. It was about panic and anxiety and the different ways to cope with it. Not really ways to get through a panic attack, but things to do when you're not in a panic attack to practice before one hits.

We all have a baseline anxiety threshold that we normally experience on a daily basis and each time we have a panic or anxiety attack it raises your baseline. There's a lot of different techniques (grounding) that help to de-stress you before you even reach the point of having an panic attack.

A lot of the points raised were extremely valuable and definitely useful. Things you would almost think were too obvious to actually work.

Our second meeting after lunch was a group recovery meeting with a recovery coach. She works with each of the units throughout the week. The meeting wasn't super helpful to me, because it was pretty much just reading an affirmation and explaining why it applied to you.

Apparently the entire rehab is completely dry, so hopefully things will slow down and be quiet for a few days. Most likely the exact opposite will happen though. Because there's nothing to get they're going to be looking harder and definitely be going through withdrawals again. As is J2 and The Giant are already going through them and two of the new girls are as well. (I haven't learned their names yet)

20 – HTTP Error Code 409

> "Hope will never be silent."
> - Harvey Milk

While working on Beyond Adversity, my faith was shaken in more ways than one. Most importantly my faith in myself. Beyond Adversity, as a movie, brings together people in a way not normally imagined. Different walks of life, different struggles, one general purpose. To heal.

When I originally read the script I didn't even read it all the way through. I only read the first few pages and got the gist of what the writer was trying to convey. A message that even through our struggles we can create something beautiful.

I signed on right away.

The entire process was hindered by my drinking. No one knew exactly what was going on, but they were buckled into a roller coaster ride of my emotions. Some days I'd be high, keeping up with all of the work that needed to get done, a positive force on the project. Others, I was much darker, deep in a drunken despair.

Originally, I thought that just by working on the project everything would get better for me. That all of a sudden I would figure out what I needed to do to get myself sober. Or at the very least not drinking.

I've never had a problem with drugs in the sense that I was mentally or physically addicted. If I wanted to stop something, I could easily walk away. That was never the case when it came to drinking.

On average, I'd drink an 18 pack of beer a day. My heaviest days of drinking I could finish a bottle of vodka by myself. My ex always knew to buy two.

Working on the film though, no one knew exactly what my problem was. My conversations were limited to the crew side, and then I was only talking to the director, a lead producer, and a social media manager that I had brought in myself.

I kept the circle small, and was close with two of the three. So I figured I would have no problem hiding my problem.

Little did I know that when you're trying to fix something you can't just follow the directions at random and hope that you'll be able to figure out the middle pieces on your own. Life is not as clear cut as IKEA directions.

My entire time working on the project, I was focused on myself, which totally missed the message of the film we were creating. We weren't just trying to help ourselves, we wanted to bring people together. Differences and all; It's what makes the film so beautiful.

Similarly, I did the same thing in rehab. You give me the steps, I'll figure out sobriety on my own. Wrong.

When you have a group of people there, willing to be a shoulder to cry on, you should use it. Life happens, things don't turn out the way you've imagined, c'est la vie.

In the end though, the broken pieces can still be mended. The puzzle may look a bit distorted, but being whole is worth the process.

21 – Finding Sobriety

> "Truth is One, Paths are Many."
> - Mahatma Gandhi

Sometimes the person you've needed to give you the push in the right direction is the last person you expect.

For me that was my sister. Her strength is what pushed me to finally take the plunge and give up everything I thought I wanted to go to rehab. At the time I thought I was going to lose everything.

When I finally got into a facility, getting sober was a lot easier than I expected. My problem was never that I needed alcohol, but that I had found a crutch to get me by in alcohol. All of my plans had kind of fallen to the wayside.

Every time I started to make strides towards achieving my goals, some sort of emotional set back would take me further into this dark place I had created for myself. The mind is a brilliant place to hide. When you layer your trauma, it becomes a sort of armor, and it allows you to fall back on it.

Rehab allowed me to forgive myself, as well as a lot of people that had faced misguided anger. The number of people

I hurt during my battle with addiction is relatively small, but I did a lot of damage in a short period of time.

My words became my shield. I could protect myself by destroying relationships before the hurt even began. Some people just liked the perks that came along with it.

I don't know how much I've given to charities, I've never kept track. I just know that when a problem arose if I had the money I would throw it at the problem, hoping someone smarter than me could fix it.

There was a struggle when I was drinking between trying to be someone that helped, and a reclusive hermit that no one really ever saw. The first time my armor slipped in a major way was my graduation party in high school.

It was the first time I had ever really had a drink with my fathers side of the family around.

Nothing major, but I'm small, and then it didn't take much for me to get drunk.

Intentionally I had hid away all of my less attractive emotions. You cry a lot when you're going through puberty at the same time as getting your first death threat.

I don't even remember how it happened. All of a sudden the school went into lock-down, I was in eighth grade and I remember all of the lights being shut off. Everyone knew my families names because of the accident, and there was a rumor going around that someone had made a list of people they didn't want at the school anymore.

Now, I have no idea if my name was really on that list, but the fact still remains. With the accident and some incidents that had happened the year before, I believed it. When you're blown up in a house, a statistic I don't even know where to begin looking for, a lot of things that seemed impossible seem possible.

Finding sobriety alone seemed just as easy once I was in. All I had to do was stick to myself, and participate in groups. I read six or seven books in my 35 days in rehab. "Murder on the Orient Express" only took me a day.

I split "The Mountain Between Us" into a few. "Great Expectations" took me the longest.

My entire time in rehab I was writing. I had gotten paper originally, but after I had filled about forty pages, I finally got a notebook.

A few people even said that if I was to ever write about my experience there, they wanted to be a part of it. Rehab allows a lot of room for growth.

In the end, my main priority was just getting myself healthy. Now a year later I've achieved something that seemed impossible for so many.

22 – Day Eight: 12 Days Sober

"The Lord is with me; I will not be afraid. What can man do to me?"
- Psalm 118:16

I didn't write nearly as much as I should have yesterday. But to share a bright moment, I got my first care package. My Grandma Savino sent two new books and a journal that says "Faith makes all things possible." Which really works out because I can keep a journal on faith related things.

Last night's AA meeting was hard to pay attention to because the Usual Suspect was sitting next to me making comments for a lot of it. There were four people, but only two that spoke. One was our first female speaker for the guys. Her name was Brave.

Brave was definitely a girl with some attitude even in sobriety. But in the best way possible she shared how she started drinking at a young age, which seems to be a reoccurring theme. It wasn't until she hit rock bottom that she was really willing to give recovery a real chance.

It all finally came to a head and her boyfriend told her she needed to leave. She had gone to an AA meeting once before but they told her the five things you should do every day.

"Screw that," she said.

Now she was homeless and she didn't know what to do. She was finally realizing all of the mistakes she had made and how she had neglected her son and considered herself a bad mother, but she knew she had to make a change.

This time when she went to AA she knew she had nothing to lose. She started doing all five things every day and started working on the twelve steps. Shes now five years sober.

With her was another guy that shared as well. All four belonged to the same group, two were just tag along's experiencing what sharing with a large group was like as a speaker.

I can't remember what his name was but his story resonated with me. He was from an upper middle class family that had a lot handed to him, His biggest problem was just not applying himself and skipping the first half of the day getting high and drunk; then spending the rest of the day screwed up at school.

I missed a lot of his story though because that's when the Usual Suspect was talking the most.

Our group before that was pretty much the 'The Leader and Usual Suspect show', they monopolized the entire meeting interrupting other people and when someone even tired to expand on what they were saying one of them would cut the others off. I'm honestly counting down the days until they leave.

Expanding on that, last night being Friday, we got to watch TV until midnight. The entire time The Leader had the remote and was in control of what we watched. The only one able to make a suggestion as to what we could watch was the Usual Suspect. The Third Musketeer and Young-One were all over each other, they're using rehab as their own personal season of the bachelor.

For the most part I don't care but at the same time it's extremely distracting.

Spirituality this morning was again really good. People opening up about moments that have affected them throughout their lives. Every unit had a pretty good showing except 'D' unit; it was no surprise but I was the only one there. It will most likely be the same thing tomorrow, but I most likely won't share, because I know people are getting sick of hearing me speak.

No one even seemed phased that they had missed the meeting, but it's getting embarrassing being the only guy representing an entire unit. People I wouldn't have expected to show up from the other wings are consistently there. Then there's us.

I don't know if it's better or worse for only one person to be there to represent 'D' wing and maybe if one person leads by example, other people will start going.

Finally I got to cut my nails and I finally got the clothes from my mom. Ashley is the one that technically picked them out for me and sent the package, but my mom paid for them which was nice.

Just putting on clean clothes I hadn't worn yet was a nice feeling and my nails were getting pretty long. Fairly successful spa day considering where we're at.

Everything since then has been drama as usual. Young-One fought with Usual Suspect about absolutely nothing, which the Third Musketeer just laughed at, which then Young-One got pissed at the Third Musketeer, which then got them fighting. Father Knowledge is his annoying self and the Leader is back to scamming how ever he can. 'D' block is a shit show.

23 — The Bond

> "All human wisdom is contained in these two words - Wait and Hope"
> - Alexandre Dumas

Every holiday season the routine is relatively the same; although there were a few years in Hollywood, that's a story for another day. All of the family gathers at my grandparents house to celebrate and be together. Having just spent a weekend learning Node and MongoDB I was thinking about more than just dinner. Our minds are just vast and complicated databases that follow no rules; SQL, NoSQL, it can do it all.

While we'd all normally be sitting around my grandmothers dining room table, this year I was shuffling screens; a global pandemic changes a few things. Although I did get to see my grandparents, there were only six of us total, my mom, her boyfriend and my great uncle included.

Thinking of how few us there were as opposed to normal, my mind wandered. Our table looked different this year, but our experience only changed slightly. Handling a friends-giving was much more complicated than one with family, but only because the relationships are so innately different. The purpose stays the same, to celebrate, but the flow of the process can be choppy based on your understanding of event planning.

In a SQL database, everything is based on relations and models. Whereas in a NoSQL database, there are no or few relationships, but definitely no schema.

My friends-givings have always included close friends, and in some ways they became sort of like a family, just the relationships aren't exactly the same.

While I lived in LA I developed a relationship with one of my next door neighbors. I even called her my LA mom. She was there for me in so many ways, including the day I almost lost my actual mother to addiction. Her oxygen levels were extremely low, so for awhile it was touch and go. Thankfully she pulled through.

Although I called her my LA mom, not every piece was there. We'd make jokes and references to how it was similar but it doesn't replace that actual mother son bond.

Our friendsgiving's always had some off the cuff people that weren't necessarily invited. Nested friendships where they were more so an acquaintance to me, but extremely important to someone I wanted there.

Due to covid though, this year everything was different. Physically, I only saw my moms side of the family and who I saw was still limited to a certain number. To talk to the rest of my family we chatted through our phones, still special, just different.

Pre-Covid our friends-giving could get huge. People would just keep showing up and we'd find a place to put them. We'd pull out extra chairs, sometimes couples would sit on each other's laps to make more room. Everyone was welcome, we'd find the space.

With the restrictions, there's nothing quite the same as being together with the people you care about. The key is following the guidelines so everyone can be safe. Similar to working with SQL.

In SQL, there are multiple different relationship types. One to one, like a parent child bond that can't be recreated. Many to one, like grandparents to a grandchild, or many to many, like cousins with multiple cousins. I'm lucky, because despite divorce, I've got a ton of family I normally get to visit.

Driving home from my grandparents is actually where I got my inspiration to start writing. In a way it was the main reason for it.

It's all about accessing your needs and the current situation. How exactly can you make the best of what you're working with? Do you need a particular person to be there? Or can you throw it together in a way you're well prepared for and make it work? Really, you just have to figure out your starting point and go from there.

24 – Day Nine: 13 Days Sober

> "I'm curious about everything. Even subjects that don't interest me."
> - Alex Trebek

I've been getting a little behind on my writing this weekend. Which really there's no excuse for, there's not been much going on group sense.

Last night in our milieu meeting we played Jeopardy. Which has kind of turned into it's own little shit show. Everyone yelling over each other, our team worked together really well though and pulled out a win.

The new girls are pretty cool. I really think I'll get along with Rehab Ashley. She seems to know J2 in some way though. So those two have been talking to each other quite a bit.

Spirituality this morning was a little bit better, we actually had four people show up. Kind of a nice surprise. J2 didn't have a lot to say, but at least there was another voice in the room.

I shared about having a family that's been addicted and how Ashley going to addiction treatment inspired me to. Just kind of focusing on how anyone could be your spark.

25 – Keyframes

> "Do, or do not. There is no try."
> - Yoda

Growing up I wanted to be a lawyer. My first real experience with one when I was 8; my mom and step-father were getting an extremely messy divorce, and there were a ton of questions about our home life. Occasional checks on our welfare, what I'd later learn is called Child Protective Services, or as my mom called them my ex-step-dads private detectives to find something wrong, which they never did.

Lawyers came in and cleaned up the mess that was left behind. Helped you pick up the pieces of what was once a family portrait, and create something new.

My father and mom were never really together; I've only ever heard one or two stories about the time they were. I know they're my parents though, because, well, hospital photos and the paternity test. This idea that there needed to be a man in the house was instilled in me when I was quite young.

Now that my sister, mom and I were all alone, I knew I had to step up.

Everything I did, I had to be better at. I had to be an example of how strong our family really is. Strong like bull is our family motto. Soccer practices became more intense. My grades needed to be straight A's. I started playing the trumpet, auditioned for the school musical, and sang our school choirs male solo parts. Whatever I needed to do to excel.

Every other weekend I'd visit my dad. When I visited him I got a taste of how the other side lived. My mom wasn't poor, but we lived paycheck to paycheck. Power only got cut off one time that I can remember. We only ran out of gas in the car on occasion. We honestly had it really easy compared to some, and I always had my books.

Second semester of Freshman year in college, during our leadership exchange program, I met a girl that hadn't learned to read until the fifth grade. She was from one of the lower income areas in Memphis, Tennessee. A city that within a few blocks distance you can see a multi-million dollar house and then on a street corner someone just setting up their cardboard apartment for the night.

To be completely honest, I don't remember much about the girl other than the fact that she hadn't learned to read until fifth grade. When my dad got married, he married a local legislators daughter. I knew the power of political rapid fire facts in a debate. At 18 I had high hopes of a political career for all of the wrong reasons.

Traumatic experiences change you. I don't care how trivial or grand of a scale, a car accident I was in where no one was hurt other than this poor deer on the highway had just as large of an impact on my life as being blown up in a house; dramatically different ways, but traumatic just the same.

For whatever reason, in my mind it was acceptable to memorize this fact but not get to know this person. Once you open up that door to caring about someone else you're opening an entrance for them as well. I've almost always worn a do not disturb sign proudly.

My biological father is a strong man. Growing up I only saw him cry a handful of times. So I've always paired that strength with the ability of not showing emotion. He taught me about money, and he always had it.

My mother is strong too, but in her own way. Ask her and she'll say she's emotional. Get to know her though and you'll see she's only vulnerable when she wants or needs to be.

Two very different youths. Two distinct struggles. But because of my selfishness I never got to know the girl from Memphis. Knowing I wasn't alone in not having the perfect white picket fence family was enough. Internally comparing survival tactics in a way to quantify our struggles I knew she had it worse.

Everything seemingly always needed a number for me to have an opinion on it. Did I do well? How expensive is it? Will that be all day?

When posed in this way, self-absorbed inside myself, I had completely missed the point. So much was going on around me but my sight never left the finish line.

Throughout the exchange we all volunteered with local charities. Samaritans feet. Feeding America. Even a local church in the Tampa Bay area. Each place we went we had an ability to make an impact.

We met people from all walks of life all with their own struggles. But I was only obsessed with the facts.

Working with Samaritans feet we were able to provide a new pair of shoes to the underprivileged kids, while also giving them a foot bath. I always made sure to ask "How'd I do?"

Feeding America was completely different. We learned about the entire process of running a non-profit focused on nutrition on the middle of a food desert. You'd never believe the cost.

On a Sunday morning at the local church in Tampa, we fed the local homeless in a sort of soup kitchen fashion.

Handing out clothes donations to whomever needed what we had available. It only lasted a few hours though, and by the end of our time there we were all asking to come back for all day events.

I didn't realize it at the time, but my biggest problem was my perception, how I was framing the things I would do. I enjoyed giving back, that was never even a question.

When you phrase the question/comment the wrong way, you're going to get a superficial answer because that's essentially what you've asked for. Chance is not change.

Have you ever woken up from a nightmare at two in the afternoon on a Friday? Not a metaphorical dream, but an actual nightmare you've placed yourself in? Not to take away any of the horrible that happened, but when you set yourself up for a victim mindset, that's exactly what you get, at least in my case.

26 – The Signal

"I need something to fill the silence."

When I started dancing, I was fifteen years old. I had done some yoga videos my Grandma had gotten from McDonald's on the TV, right around that time they also got the Wii fit. Guided movement allows you to get a sense of your appendages, each individual piece of yourself like a brush on a canvas, a pen on the page.

Through this movement you can learning breathing techniques and placement. Pas de bourree, pas de bourree, fouette, fouette, fouette into oblivion, a top spinning on a table, your body becoming the instrument.

In Waitomo village, there is a glow worm cave excursion called the Black Abyss at Black Water Rafting. As part of the package with the Kiwi Experience I was able to go spelunking with a group of strangers. If you've ever seen the movie the Descent that's exactly how the excursion started. Rappelling 150 meters deep into the ground. Meanwhile, I'm four beers deep.

Sinking into that cavern there should have been a certain sense of fear. But instead I felt invincible, those beers giving a sort of social confidence I don't normally have. I had made friends with the girls of the group and their boyfriends.

"You can go first," I told each them as they dropped into an hour glass shaped crevice.

Legs shaking my harness was strapped in, slowly sinking, bounce, bounce, the rig and line were stuck. In the middle of the hour glass, I could feel the guide bounce the line and I drop a few feet 90 meters in the air.

Arriving at the bottom the wet suits and gear we were given to wear made sense, masks and flashlight LED helmets. All there as a sense of security in this deep underground unknown.

Our guide takes the lead.

"You'll have to squeeze through this crevice, we're going down before we go up."

"We zip line next, right," Phil asks?

At one hundred and twenty five pounds, I needed to use the water in the cavern to get leverage squeezing through the nooks and crannies. Some of the guys must have been having real trouble I thought to myself as I slowly fell to the back of the pack.

The zip line was another 50 meter descent, and to enjoy it our guide suggested turning our lamps off. Zipping through the sky in a pitch black cavern with glow worms is quite an experience.

Coming to the bottom the water started to get deeper. At this point about shin deep. The wet suit keeping all of the heat in, despite the depth I was feeling toasty.

Next up was a tubing experience where you jump from a cliff about 20 meters high followed by pulling yourself and others by rope into the deepest part of the cavern, at this point about 300 meters deep.

"Shut off your lights and you'll really get to see the glow worms."

Seven lights click off, as our guide slowly pulls the chain of us on our tubes back the way we came from.

"By this point your arms are probably burning but the best part is yet to come. Now that it's dark thousands of glow worms will light up."

"They're beautiful," I said.

Slowly careening back through the caverns you couldn't help but stare in amazement. Beautiful creatures, as if slowly coming to life, emitting a beautiful light blue glow. The walls beginning to patch together in clusters of worms, as if an abstract painting being created in front of our eyes.

By this point in the tour the only thing let to do was climb up and out. My brave had worn off when I almost jumped to my death during a belly flop stop.

"Don't jump towards me there are shallow rocks, and don't jump towards the ladder you'll get stuck," our guide said as I turned the corner, too far away and tipsy to hear.

Deep below the Earths surface, body fueled by corona's for breakfast and screwdrivers for dinner, my only means of escape relying on my physical strength. In a moment like that, you truly face your maker. You would think a wake up call in some sense.

My legs have always been the strongest part of me. From years of soccer, track, and dance. But in this cavern I needed upper body strength.

Body shaking I remember getting to the light. I had found a new hobby. I was a spelunker.

27 — The Pin

CONTENT WARNING
Graphic Content

Losing Jay was just the beginning of a horrible week for me. There were multiple consecutive failures so quickly. I'm not sure exactly how someone hacks a machine, but it was as if someone had taken away all of the security, skydiving without a parachute almost.

The day I found out about Jay, I broke. Not just for myself, but for everyone that knew her. When I told my family they were supportive, but upset that I was going to cut my time on vacation with them short to go to the funeral.

Standing on the balcony my father said to me "Well, if that's really what's most important to you."

It was never that it was more, or the most, important for me to go to the funeral versus spending time with them, I just hadn't realized you could say good bye without having to do it publicly. Saying goodbye in private makes it just for you.

Arriving in Florida, I knew around about where the funeral was being held. There was a manatee leadership retreat where you got to swim with them right around the same area. Landing in Orlando I picked up a friend and we splurged while shopping.

Having an addictive personality makes it easy to get hooked on one thing to the next because your mind is always seeking that next great high. Swimming with manatees just as rewarding serotonin wise as a shopping spree.

I purchased some luggage but barely anything to go in them. Finding expensive clothes in the wrong sizes. Most set in my closet with tags never being pulled off, later sold to second hand shops for quick cash and a bottle of vodka for the night.

My drinking all started heavily on that trip to Florida. Staying in a hotel that cost way too much and more than enough room for twice the amount of people. I started to cave myself in. As long as I wasn't driving I could be drinking.

My first gay pride that weekend I still felt out of place. Although I had dealt with my internal stigmas I still felt out of place. I had spent the entire year fighting for rights on campus, taking an LGBT culture course, yet inside something felt off.

After going to Jay's funeral there were still so many questions about what had happened. Personally, I stayed out of those discussions because I already felt as if I was responsible.

On the last night of my trip, I decided to go to Orlando with some of guy friends. I always thought Candy Man had a crush on me, I'd later be stuck in a love triangle between him and Storybook.

While we were getting ready I made sure not to step out to smoke a cigarette. Back then I had far better impulse control hiding secrets. I drank a 24 oz, possibly 40 oz bud light and then I blacked out. I don't remember much more about that night.

Ayn Rand has this analogy for cigarettes, and how you hold the power of the world in your finger tips with the butt of the cigarette being a flame. I don't know what happened to me that night though. So I shouldn't say I'm a survivor.

Finally getting on the plane the next day, I sat gingerly. On the sixth of July, the following day, my mom, sister and I were going to meet my cousin and great aunt in San Juan Puerto Rico. Getting there we were surprised to learn Runner Runner was filming in the casino.

When I explained what happened, my mom called it rape. "You should get tested. Also, I may need some help while we're in Puerto Rico."

Having seen Law and Order SVU so many times I knew that I'd showered off any DNA and I'm pretty sure I never saw those clothes again. Plus we were going zip lining in Puerto Rico, I couldn't miss that.

Looking back now it's like I never stopped zip-lining in Puerto Rico. Zip-lining in New Zealand happened so many years later, but I was still stuck in that same mindset, still stuck in a cave.

On that trip in Puerto Rico is when my alcoholism really started. But as a symptom of avoiding years of PTSD coupled with a new inciting incident.

With treatment I've been able to start facing these issues, but it has been a long drawn out process, one that will take time.

I've spent a lot of time in my life blaming other people when really my problems lie within. Now is the time to live as who I want to be, not as who I've forced myself to be.

Afterword

> "It's not abnormal for a lifetime of trauma and anxiety to make the recovery process a long one."
> - Jessica Pike

The day of release for this book tentatively marks one year of sobriety for me. The first time I had the idea to write a book, I was probably 8 years old. It essentially was what is today fan-fiction of the dot Hack series season one. What I didn't know was that I was writing about the future me.

Addiction takes something from you that unless you've struggled with it you can't fully understand. You are honestly trapped in your own body with your worst desires 24/7. Combine that with co-occurring mental health issues, you become a bit of an eclectic person with out even trying. You find the cracks you fit in, and you do what you can to survive.

For a long time, I had to live as if my life were scripted just to survive, it was a part of being in an abusive relationship, as well as having medical problems that come out nowhere. You learn to say you're okay, even when you're not.

To be honest, I structured the contents of the book very loosely. I wanted them to seem like journal entries because that's essentially what they are. Everything from rehab is exactly as written in my journals, except for where the sentence made absolutely no sense, I left it this way because in my mind at that time all I could think about was surviving. The chapters are meant to play off of one another and there's a ton of references to all sorts of different movies and pop culture.

There's so many people, and so many things I wish I could have fit into this book. But I'm trying something new where I actually follow through on the things I say I'm going to do. I've wanted to publish something for years, but never felt I had something that was quite ready. Although it's missing a lot, it covers the parts of my story I want to be told. The parts that people wouldn't mention.

Mental health has been taboo for too long, and needs the awareness more now than ever. But by not speaking about the things that hurt us, aren't we only giving them more power? I'm extremely influenced by Kierkegaard, and like him, my first book is just catch up. There will be more to come, the future is full of hope.

- ZP

Made in the USA
Middletown, DE
21 March 2021